D0200473

A Boy's Summer

A Boy's Summer

FATHERS AND SONS TOGETHER

Gerry Spence

Illustrations and Inclusions
by Tom Spence

St. Martin's Press New York

www.stmartins.com

Book design by Donna Sinisgalli
Production Editor: David Stanford Burr

Library of Congress Cataloging-in-Publication Data

Spence, Gerry.
     A boy's summer : fathers and sons together / by Gerry Spence ; illustrations
  and inclusions by Tom Spence.
        p.   cm.
     ISBN 0-312-20282-2
     1. Fathers and sons.   2. Boys—Recreation.   3. Family recreation.
  4. Outdoor recreation.   I. Title.

HQ755. 85.S67 2000
306.874'2—dc21   00-024144

First Edition: June 2000

10   9   8   7   6   5   4   3   2   1

To our father:

    Who played with us,

    Danced and sang

    The songs of life with us

    In those endless days of summer.

    It was, we thought,

    A better way

    To speak of love.

    And to our sons, and theirs.

Contents

An Introduction for Fathers

That we have written a book about fathers and sons rather than parents and children seems to ignore the fact that approximately half of the parental population of this country is made up of mothers, and half the children are girls. Yet we sometimes overlook the obvious; That boys and girls, fathers and mothers, and their relationships to each other, are different, and that the difference is not only genetic but healthy—indeed, divine. Because the relationships are different, they need to be celebrated in their own context. Therefore it seemed to us that we would be more likely to hit the mark if we dealt with one relationship at a time. Since my brother, Tom, and I are also fathers of girls, we have reserved the right to a later book about the inimitable relationship of fathers and daughters.

At eight—yes, still at fourteen—the relationship of father and son in its idyllic state is an intimacy between God and boy. Seeing a father change course and seek to correct an error, to say, "I am sorry—let's try again" and mean it, allows the relationship to become richer. Yet to their sons, most often fathers appear incapable of wrong. They stand omnipotent beyond all human capacity. They seem wholly wise, wonderful and brave. They are, at last, a boy's first true friend, for true friends stand ready to share, to love and to protect against a hostile world.

No school teaches us how to become successful human beings, no college course is titled, "How to Become a Person." It's from fathers that boys learn the important lessons about being men. Both Tom and I were constantly with our father, hunting and fishing, exploring, creating, and rejoicing in what he called "God's real church," the out-of-doors. And in that church and in his company we learned many important lessons. We are privileged to pass some of them on to you and your son, at last the best evidence of immortality that I know of.

What do we fathers want for our sons? As for me, the father of four sons, and Tom, the father of two, we have wanted our sons to become aware of the world around them, to be curious, to become acquainted with themselves, and to be responsible and joyously creative. We have wanted them to grow up under a better influence than that provided by the relentless and insidious psychological attack of the corporate nanny: television and video games. We have wanted our sons to know how to think for themselves, to ask important questions, to learn how to entertain themselves, to become splendidly at ease with themselves and with the earth. We have wanted

them to grow up honest in this profoundly dishonest world, to have ideals that are rich and meaningful as distinguished from the grossly acquisitive and greedy values of the society in which we live. We have wanted them to be tolerant of their fellowman and to see success as a measure of the evolution of the person, not the growth of bank accounts. Both Tom and I are grateful to our sons who, by having fulfilled our expectations of them as sons, have permitted us to fulfill our goals for ourselves as fathers.

As adults we judge every event in our lives against the primary experiences of our childhoods. If we have been provided those wondrous times of father and son, of creating and playing, of experimenting and exploring, we carry these formative experiences into manhood and daily test our lives and judgments against them. But if our primary experiences have been the violence of the vacuous tube, the canned laughter and the empty-headed cartoons, if television has instructed us what to eat, what to wear, what to buy and, alas, what to think, we can surely predict the resulting values we will have as men. We would not knowingly deliver our children to a psychopathic baby-sitter. Yet with little hesitation we too often yield to the corporate companion, TV, video games, and the Internet, which, void of any conspicuous conscience, daily molds the minds of our children.

Ought not our sons, instead, more often have their roots soaked in the good earth of garden and forest, of park and prairie? Ought not our children grow from foundational experiences—of tying a fly and catching a fish, of making a kite, digging a cave and writing a poem? The primary experiences of boys should include the exciting outings of fathers and sons roaming, building, learning, discovering, creating and playing together. Boys should learn that their fathers are also boys, and that together as boys they can traipse though basement, backyard and woods, explore the countryside, the mountains and the prairies. These experiences together represent the species at last returning to the tribe, where fathers prevail as the teachers of their sons. Besides, it is fun to be a father, because good fatherhood is in the end but a reversion to responsible boyhood.

Ah, to be ten again, to be real as a new potato, as innocent as tulips, to wear no social mask disguising who we are, to be pure as fresh sap from the pine and curious as a pup, to be able to laugh because it feels good and to run whenever the delight of running demands. I say we should always be boys, that we should never grow up. Not really. Not in the heart. Not in our creativity, not in our love of life, our curiosity, our need to ask questions, to take risks and to forever remain open to new learning.

This book, then, is for boys and their fathers, fathers who want again to be boys and boys who want to grow up like their fathers. This book is for boys who, with their fathers, will share those precious moments that create the stuff of a lifetime from which successful sons and, because of them, successful fathers are made.

GERRY SPENCE

JACKSON, WYOMING

An Introduction for Sons

Fathers are just boys with whiskers.

Fathers are like tree trunks. Ever look at a tree trunk cut straight through so you can see all the rings? Go look at a stump. You'll see that at the very center of the tree is the tiniest circle, which was once the sapling, the baby tree. Like you, each year the tree grew a little and left its ring of growth behind until all the rings together made the full-grown tree. The tree has leaves on the outside. Fathers have whiskers. And some have hair. But inside both the tree and the father is the sapling—the boy.

It's nice to know this about fathers. Their voices may be louder and deeper. They are, of course, taller and stronger than boys. Like a tree they have stood against many a storm and have seen many a hard time. They have learned a lot and, to be sure, have a lot more to learn. They often play in different ways than boys and do different work. But even though they may

sometimes look and act and sound different than you, in their hearts, at the center, they are still boys—like you. So fathers can be pals just as boys of your own age are pals. All fathers have to do is go down into the tree of themselves and find the sapling. Can you explain that to your father?

But a father is also a father, which is not like being a boy at all. A father has great responsibilities, the greatest of which is to be a good father, to show his son how to grow up to become a successful person. It is not easy to be a father. A father worries about his son. He's afraid something will happen to his boy, that he will be injured. And a boy can be injured in more than one way. For instance, a boy can be run over in the street. But a boy can also be injured by being with the wrong kinds who lead the boy into wrong ways. Gangs, for instance. Kids who are on drugs, for instance. Kids who get in trouble with the law, for instance. To be a father is sometimes very frightening for fathers.

Although fathers have great power, so do sons. A son can make the job of the father very easy or very hard. If a son loves his father, he will make the father's job as easy as he can. And a son can do this by saving his father from worry, by doing his homework, by getting home on time, by not keeping company with boys who do wrong things. A boy can make his father a successful father by becoming a successful boy, or he can keep the father from being a successful father by doing wrong things. So sons have power and therefore a large responsibility to fathers.

This book is to help you help your father to be a successful father, and to help him help you to become a successful son. He wants to be with you, to do things with you, to be a boy again with you and, at the same time, to become a successful father. He wants you to learn how much he loves you. The best way for you to know how much he loves you, of course, is for him to spend time with you, for the two of you to do things together that are fun—

like the things in this book—things that you will remember when you, yourself, are someday a father and have a son of your own.

Helping your father become a successful father by being a successful son is fun. So go get your father and say, "Let's go do something together. Your work can wait 'til tomorrow. You need to be with me today so I can help you be a good dad." Besides, you might tell him, "I need you to be my best friend."

GERRY SPENCE

JACKSON, WYOMING

How to Use This Book

One of the purposes of this book is to provide a father the opportunity to read to his son *and the son to his father.* This book is meant to be read aloud. The book itself would feel disappointed if it were mumbled over, if it caused only silent lips to get tired in the reading, if, indeed, the wonderful sounds of a boy reading to his father, and vice versa, were kept from the ears of either. Boys should be read to by fathers and fathers by sons. That is part of the togetherness that brings on the magic.

Which of these pages should be read by the father and which by the son? It makes little difference. For instance, "A Mouse in the House" is written for the son to read. It suggests how the son might misbehave slightly as part of learning about how to impose one's presence on others with style through the art of entertainment. But it would also be fun for the father to read the boy's secret so that, at last, there are no secrets between father and son.

And one other thing: In this father-son experience, these projects must be done with a father's supervision. We do not dig a cave without the father seeing that it is safely braced. We do not build a tree house, especially the one Tom drew, without recognizing the danger in climbing up and down, both while building it and playing in it. Being exposed to lightning while flying a kite, falling, drowning, all are potential dangers. But that is part of the experience—discovering the dangers and dealing with them safely. Don't rely on the drawings to tell you what is deemed safe. Rely on your own common sense. Helping your son form sound judgments is part of his growing up into a successful man.

This being said, let us go out into the world, out into the mountains and the countryside, out into the parks, out even into the backyard or the basement. Let us get up, go out, and create a life for ourselves.

1

Into the Wind—Making a Kite

SPRINGTIME, THE wind, a boy, his father and a kite all belong together. In the spring, the wind blows, sometimes as if to blow away the memories of winter. But so far as I can figure out, the wind in the spring is for only one purpose, and that's for a boy and his father to fly a kite.

Boys and fathers have been flying kites since the day that string was invented. Some say a Greek scientist by the name of Archytas of Tarentum invented the kite five hundred years before Christ was born. But the ancient Chinese had been flying kites even before that. And every spring during all of those thousands of years the wind was blowing. And boys had fathers. So the point is that boys and fathers flying kites in the spring is part of being human. It's in our genes, as it's in the genes of fish to swim and birds to fly. Man himself has always wanted to fly, and before he invented flying machines, flying kites was about as close as he could come to it. So there's no getting around it—you and your dad have to make a kite and fly it.

You can buy a kite, of course. In fact, you can buy some very fancy ones. Even when I was a boy you could go to the dime store and buy a kite. But they were usually flimsy or didn't fly very well, and they cost something like twenty-five cents, and in those days that was a lot of money. They were never as good as the ones my dad and I used to make. Besides, who would want to buy a kite when you can make one? Making a kite is more than half the fun—thinking about how it's going to fly and whether we're as smart as the Greeks and the Chinese.

What materials and tools do we need to make this little flying machine? We need some sticks and some plain, two-foot-wide wrapping paper; some paste (Elmer's glue will work); and some old cotton rags, perhaps from an old dress or apron. And, of course, a lot of kite string—the more you have, the higher you can fly the kite. For tools, we need a saw, a pocketknife to whittle the sticks and a pair of scissors. That's all.

Now, about the sticks: Look around the house for some old boards or split firewood with straight grain. Fir is the best, but you could use other straight-grained wood. The wood you choose should be sawed to about thirty inches in length before you split off the sticks. Now split off three sticks. Make them about half an inch in diameter and whittle them nice and smooth. Two of the sticks will be about thirty inches long. The

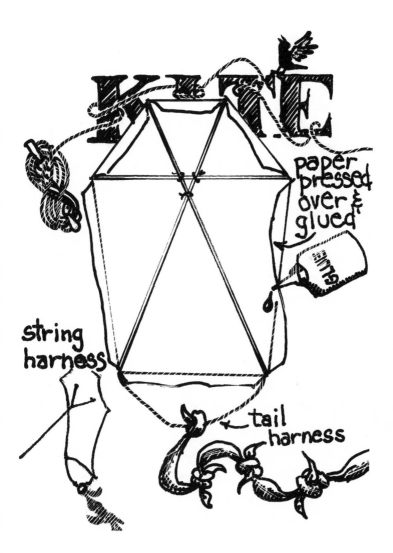

KITE

paper
pressed
over &
glued

string
harness

tail
harness

third stick will be about twenty-four inches. (They can be a little shorter or longer. Just keep the length of the sticks in proportion to each other, as shown in Tom's drawing.)

About a quarter of an inch from both ends of each stick, make a very tiny notch all the way around—but not deep enough to weaken the stick. These notches will hold the framing string in place. Now cross the longer sticks to make an X as shown, with the top of the X smaller than the bottom. You don't have to be a rocket scientist to do this. Just place the sticks to look as much like the drawing as possible. Next, take some kite string and bind these sticks together. Then place the shortest of the three sticks across the X as shown in the drawing, and bind that stick to the other two. This creates two more places to tie, which will make the kite frame strong.

You now have the frame together—it's that easy. With string that is somewhat stronger than kite string (we used cotton grocery-store string), and starting at the right upper limb of the frame, tie the string to the notch and then stretch the string from one limb to the next, looping the string around the limb's notch two or more times. Then go to the next limb, loop the string around the notch there, and so on until you have gone completely around the kite ending where you started. You can glue the string at the notches if you like. Now your kite frame is ready to paper.

Place the wrapping paper on the floor and lay the kite frame over it. Cut the paper about an inch wider than the outline of the kite. Then simply fold the paper back over the string, trim the paper where needed, and glue as shown in the drawing. Now you have it! The kite! The flying machine made by you. All we have to do is make the harnesses and pray for wind.

Let's make the harness for the kite string. The easiest way to make this harness is to punch a small hole through the paper at the exact center of the crosspiece. Then, from the face of the kite, thread the string back through the hole and tie the string to the exact center of the crosspiece. Or you can make a string harness as shown in Tom's drawing. What we are trying to do is create an angle of flight so that when the tail of the kite is attached (which holds the bottom of the kite down) the top of the kite is tipped forward against the pull of the kite string. When the wind hits the kite at this angle, the kite climbs as it tries to get away from the string to fly free with the wind—and in the trying, it continues to climb to the end of the string.

While we are dealing with the kite string, let's unwind the kite string from the ball onto a stick about a foot long, winding the string diagonally back and forth on the stick. We can let out string faster from the stick than from the ball. Besides, we need several balls of string because we want to fly the kite high—oh, as high as we can until it's hard to see it way up there.

Now let's make the tail. Take a cotton rag (cut off all the hems first for easy tearing) and tear the cotton into strips two to three feet in length and a couple of inches wide. Tie the ends of the strips together until you have a tail five or six feet long. Now secure a loop of strong string between the two bottom limbs, as shown. Tie the tail in the center of this loop. Experiment with the tail length. The proper length depends upon how heavy the tail is compared to the strength of the wind and the weight of the kite. Assuming a fair wind, the kite will fly straighter and climb faster with a longer tail than a shorter one. If it fights too hard to get off the ground, shorten the tail. If, after the kite is in the air, it goes around and around in a crazy fashion, you don't have enough tail to properly weight the kite so that it assumes the correct angle against the wind.

Let's go fly this baby! Find a place without trees, power lines, or telephone poles or other obstructions—a large open park or a field. *It is dangerous to fly a kite around power lines because the string could be damp and conduct a killer current down the string into your body.* Besides, we don't want our kite caught in the wires, because that would be the end of it. Good-bye kite. And good-bye a lot of good string. Never climb a pole to free your kite. Give it up and make another one.

Unwind about twenty or thirty feet of string. Have Dad hold the kite up, the face of the kite into the wind. The two of you may have to run together to get it up in the air if the wind is light. This is the time for you to judge the length of the tail. Nothing very hard about all of this. It will come naturally once you go out and do it and experiment a little. Benjamin Franklin used a kite with a key attached to the string and flew it in a lightning storm to demonstrate that the nature of lightning is electrical. *Don't do this!* He could have been electrocuted if his string had been wet. What you and your dad want to do is just have fun. See the kite fly—no motor, no propellant except the wondrous spring wind. Only the lovely wind, a boy, his dad and a kite. What could be better? And remember, when someone in a sassy voice tells you, "Go fly a kite," you can say, with great happiness, "OK." Then run for your room where your kite is hanging on the wall.

G.S.

2

Walking on Stilts

THE DIFFERENCE between you and this magical tall guy named Michael Jordan who plays basketball and gets a lot of money for selling things on TV (that cost a lot more because he's selling them) is that he has a built-in pair of stilts that he walks around on all of the time.

If you want to be as tall as he is, it's very easy to arrange. All we have to do is make a pair of stilts, and there's nothing much to that. You can see how to do it from Tom's picture (see page 9).

For the foot-blocks, take a two-by-four-inch block and saw it diagonally. This will give you the two foot-blocks you need. Better to screw them into the stilts than nail them. Stronger. The straps over the feet can be of any strong strapping material you can find. Nail the straps to the stilt. The straps shouldn't be too tight, so you can pull your feet out if you fall, which you

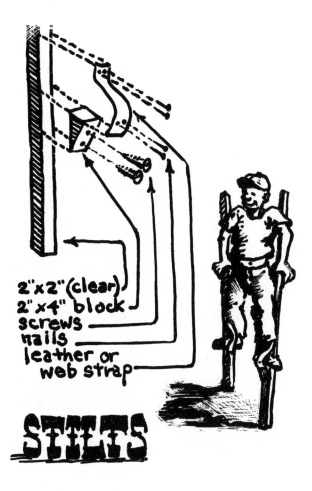

2"x2" (clear)
2"x4" block
screws
nails
leather or
    web strap

STILTS

probably will the first few times. Be sure that the two-by-twos that you use for the stilts have been smoothed with sandpaper, because you want to save your hands from splinters.

The question is, how do you learn to walk on these things?

When I started to learn my father put the foot-blocks right down next to the ground. I thought that was a sissy thing to do and I hollered and pouted about it, but I learned to walk on them at that level very easily. Not only do you have to learn to get up on the stilts, but you have to get off of them as well—without falling. You can learn to mount the stilts by putting in one foot first, and as you step up, put your other foot in the other stilt. If you learn to do this with the foot-blocks low to the ground and get good at mounting and dismounting, and if you also get good at walking on them, then you and Dad can raise the blocks a little higher, and when you get good at the next height you can raise them still higher. I finally had the foot-blocks at the same height as the front steps on the porch, which was a couple of feet high. Then I climbed up the steps, moved the stilts over to the side of the steps and mounted the stilts.

This is another activity in which you need to use some care. Pay attention to what you're doing and where you step. You can fall off the stilts and break a bone. If you are walking on a very wet lawn, the bottom of the stilts will dig into the grass, and this might not only damage the lawn but also cause you to fall. It's a good idea to practice on a lawn that has dried, so that when you fall you have a little cushion under you.

When you're first learning to walk with the foot-blocks down low, practice falling. Practice pushing down on your stilts with your hands as you begin to fall and kick free. Find the safest way to get free of the stilts as the fall begins. You will learn from experience the best way to take care of yourself. Don't go too high until you are good and safe at what you do. Always do your experimenting while you are close to the ground.

Now, walking on stilts teaches us something. We are the same person whether we are up high on stilts or not. Long legs that make a person tall do not make the person smarter or better or more brave or more beautiful. A tall person, someone bigger than you, is just another person walking on his built-in stilts. Except he can't get out of his, and you can.

G.S.

3

Making a Whistle

WHETHER YOU are an Indian in the woods or a boy on the
street, you need a whistle. That's because whistles and boys go
together like pancakes and syrup. What kind of a boy would
you be if you didn't know how to make a whistle? You would be
"plum ignorant," as Tom Sawyer would say. Yet ask any boy if
he knows how to make a whistle and he'll probably tell you no.

If you are in the woods and things are very still, very quiet,
and you are all alone, it's nice to have a whistle to make sure
that you are there. You have heard the old conundrum.* If a
tree falls in the forest and no one is there to hear it, does it

---

* A conundrum is sort of like a riddle. Sometimes there is an answer and sometimes not. As often as not the answer doesn't make any sense. Sometimes the
answer just asks another question.

make a sound? Well, if a boy is in the forest alone without a whistle, and he hollers, and no one is there to hear him, did he holler? Yet if the boy has a whistle, everybody knows that a whistle makes a noise whenever you blow on it. Does this make any sense? And if it does or doesn't, why?

When you are in the woods with Dad and you are separated and can't see each other, it's nice to have a whistle to let him know where you are. And he can have one too and whistle back, and that way you can walk through the woods whistling back and forth like a couple of happy birds, and what is more fun than that? There is something very holy about woods that are so large and so silent. Woods are to be respected, as we are respectful in church or in a library. You don't holler or talk loud in a church or a library because there's something that makes us feel reverent about such places. You whisper when you're there.

Boys and dads ought not to yell at each other in the woods or talk loud. It disturbs the woods. The woods like softer sounds, the sounds of the chipping squirrel or the occasional chatter of a jay, the warble of a song bird or the sweet call of the forest thrush or even the distant howl of the coyote or the quick yapping of the fox. Deer rarely make a sound. The elk lives in the forest, and except during the mating season, is mostly silent as a statue. Forest creatures are very respectful of the great cathedral in which they live, so that often you can walk through the woods and hear only the powerful shouting of silence. But

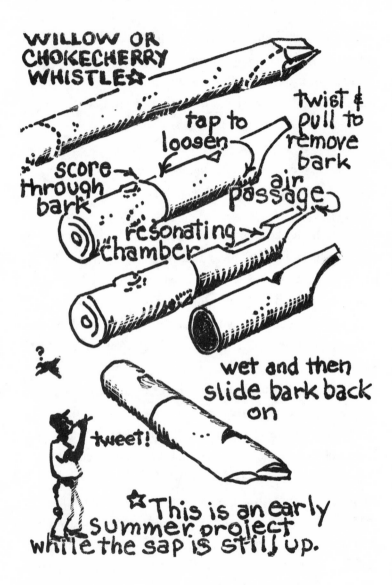

WILLOW OR CHOKECHERRY WHISTLE☆

tap to loosen

twist & pull to remove bark

score through bark

air passage

resonating chamber

wet and then slide bark back on

tweet!

☆This is an early summer project while the sap is still up.

when we have a willow whistle we can blow on it as we go and its sound will blend with the other forest sounds so as not to disturb the woods.

How do we make a whistle? We wander along the stream in the springtime with Dad looking for a willow or a chokecherry bush. In the springtime the sap has come up to prepare the bush to burst into the bloom of flower and leaf, and it's the sap right under the bark that will permit us to remove the bark in one piece, which is the secret to making a whistle.

First, find a length of branch about five inches long. It ought to be free of any little limbs or sprouts, and should be about the size of your father's third finger. The reason we don't want any limbs or sprouts coming out of the bark is that when we wrest the bark from the section of limb we have cut, little holes will be left where the limb or sprout used to be, and we don't want any holes in the bark except the ones we cut.

Now, cut one end of the limb to form the whistle end—the mouthpiece (see Tom's drawing, left). Note, we not only cut the end at a diagonal for the mouthpiece, but we also trim the end of the diagonal so that instead of it coming to a point we cut a small flat section off the end, leaving a blunt point that we will later trim out. Again, see Tom's drawing. Next, about an inch and a half back from the mouthpiece, cut a V-shaped notch through the bark and into the wood beneath. This notch should be fairly deep, maybe a quarter of an inch deep and a quarter of an inch wide.

Then, about an inch from the blunt end of the whistle,

make a circular score through the bark. Cut all the way around the limb through the bark. With the handle end of your pocket knife, tap sharply all around the section between the cut and the end of the mouthpiece, tapping the bark hard enough to loosen it from the wood, but not hard enough to break the surface of the bark. The tapping and tapping around and around this section is the key to loosening the bark from the wood. Then just twist the bark loose from the limb and slide it off— just like that. See the green, wet wood underneath?

From the tip of the mouthpiece to the notch, cut in the air space. Tom's drawing shows it. Trim out the air space and the resonating chamber, a little at a time. Experiment by slipping the bark back on and blowing. If no whistling sound comes, slip the bark back off and trim some more. Usually the resonating chamber needs adjustment. Whittle at it until you get it right. Don't make the air passage too large, but just large enough to allow an ample amount of air through. You will probably have to deepen the V cut a little as well. Work at the V and the air space until the whistle finally sounds. You might have to make a second whistle in the process of learning. It's all a matter of trial and error, but once you have the hang of it, you can make a whistle in a matter of a few minutes. Then off you go through the woods, respecting the silence, but whistling once in a while like a bird to that other bird over there who is your dad.

G.S.

4

How to Make an Argument–for a Pup (or Something Else?)

LEARNING HOW to make a successful argument is a very important skill, because an argument is just a way of convincing someone about something that interests us. Arguing is communicating in a more powerful way. And we will be making arguments all of our lives. The more successful we become at making arguments, the more successful we will become as persons. So, to illustrate how we can make a winning argument, let's make an argument for one of the most important things a boy can ever own—a dog. If you already have a dog, you can help a friend who doesn't by helping him make an argument for his dog.

Every boy should have a dog—that is the *premise*, or what

we are arguing for—and in making our argument, whether we already own a dog or not, we can learn how important having one really is to us and to our families.

To make an argument that is powerful—one that will win—we have to talk to ourselves first. I talk to myself all the time. People who do not talk to themselves must be pretty lonely and pretty strange, because if you want to know somebody, you have to talk to them, and how can you know yourself if you don't talk to yourself? So we have to go sit down somewhere and ask questions of ourselves, like: How come dogs are so important to us human beings? And why? What are dogs good for, anyway? What is our history with dogs? Why do some people love dogs more than they love people? Questions like that.

When we find the answers to these questions, we will be prepared to make our argument for a dog, and being prepared is the most important part of making any argument. It's like getting ready to take a trip. You have to have your food and extra clothes, and you have to know where you're going and how you're going to get there, or you might get lost out in the wilderness. In the same way, you need to prepare for your argument so you don't get stuck in the middle of the argument without the answers, and then lose your argument.

We should start with a little history, because as President Harry Truman once said, "There is nothing new in the world except the history you do not know." So what is our human history with dogs? Look under "dog" in the encyclopedia. You will find some wonderful and exciting information about how dogs have been man's (and boy's) best friend from the time we were living in caves. You could argue from our history that we have loved dogs for so long, and they have become such a part of our lives, that our love for them is in our genes as it is in the genes of birds to nest in the spring and fly south in the fall.

Dogs and human beings, and especially dogs and boys, belong together. They depend upon each other. The word for that is "symbiotic," which is a word that means—well, look it up, because when you learn this word you can find a lot of uses for it. An example: You can say, "Dad, we have a *symbiotic relationship,*" and that will cause your father's mouth to drop open and to look at you strangely, and that is fun, too—to make fathers' mouths drop open in surprise.

Back to the business of dogs: Dogs and human beings have depended upon each other about as long as man has wandered around on this earth. Dogs can smell things we can't smell. They can hear things we can't hear. They can tell us when danger is approaching. They can guard us. They have herded our sheep and goats and cattle. They have hunted game for us so we don't starve. They retrieve our ducks if we are duck hunters, and provide eyes for those who are blind, plus all of the other things you have learned from the encyclopedia about our history with dogs.

But let me give you some other arguments to make—arguments which, if you have been talking to yourself, you have probably already thought of. If we have a dog, we must learn to train him, to teach him those manners that will make the dog a gentleman. In training a dog we teach ourselves patience and kindness and learn how to be gentlemen ourselves. We learn to be firm but just. We learn to be responsible, because a dog trusts us, and we must never betray that trust. But a dog must have a boy as well. A dog must have a boy who will care for him, who will love him, who will be sure he is fed and kept healthy. So by now we know what a *symbiotic relationship* is, don't we? It is one in which we need each other, right? Like a father and a son, like a boy and his dog.

These are important lessons for a boy to learn. Every parent wants his boy to be patient and kind and trustworthy and responsible—parents are very *vulnerable* here, which means that your parents want very badly for you to learn such things. So your arguments about how you will learn patience and kindness and responsibility will carry great weight with them. That is an important thing to know about making a successful argument: Find what the other person wants, and then show that person how what you are arguing for will help provide the thing the person wants.

Arguments are made stronger by quoting someone who is supposed to know more than we do—perhaps even more than the person we are arguing to. (Remember, I quoted Harry Truman about history.) We call people who are supposed to know more than we do "authorities." People who write books are

sometimes seen as authorities, whether they know very much or not. So you might find it handy to quote me as an authority, because I'm right here, and you can say, "Gerry Spence says..." And here's what I say about learning from dogs: I have learned more from my dogs than I have from most of the supposed wise men I have encountered in the world. A dog teaches us to love. It teaches us how to be a friend, to accept our friend even if sometimes the friend makes mistakes—just as our dog accepts us even when we do things that are unjust or careless or thoughtless, things that might even hurt our dog. Still, our dog, like a good friend, forgives us and loves us just the same. That is a very big thing to learn—how to be a faithful friend. A dog teaches us that better than most human beings can.

A dog teaches us to ask for what we want. If a dog wants to be loved, to be petted, he comes over and puts his head on your lap or stops and looks up into your face with those eyes and whines a little to say, "Love me, pet me." He doesn't go off in the corner and pout like some people do when they don't get what they want. He just asks for what he wants, in an honest way, and that is a good thing that our dog teaches us to do—to be straight about what we want so people know and don't have to guess, so we don't have to play senseless, painful games with each other.

In making an argument, it is sometimes good to tell a story. People like stories, and to tell a story that proves a point in your argument makes your argument interesting and stronger. Let me show you: I want to argue that dogs are brave and that a boy can learn bravery from a dog. So let me tell you a story about Sam, our black lab. When he was just a pup he followed me down to the corral where we were working the cattle. The old cows were in the corral with their calves, and cows are very protective of their calves as your parents are protective of you. And along came Sam, just bouncing along after me, not knowing anything about how serious old cows were about protecting their calves, and suddenly this old cow saw Sam. And she started to snort at Sam, and before he even knew what had happened she'd chased him into a boarded-up corner in the corral where he couldn't get out. Now, Sam wasn't any bigger to that cow than you would be to an elephant, and a big elephant at that. And the cow was going to crush him with her head right there in the corner of the corral, and I couldn't get to him in time. But that pup, about six months old, turned into the most ferocious beast I ever saw. He pulled back his lips and he bared his teeth and he let out the most frightening snarl after snarl. And that old cow saw this beast who was going to bite her nose off, and she backed away just a little, just enough for Sam to get out of there. Right then and there I learned how brave dogs can be—even a pup—and I learned from Sam that sometimes we, too, have to be brave to survive in this world.

The thing is, people are always trying to train dogs to be part human. But I think we should let our dogs train us to be part dog.

A good argument also includes something that touches the heart, the "wonderful heart-stuff" let's call it. Here's an example: There is something about a dog in the house that is magic. It turns a house into a home. I call it "dogness." (It is all right to make up words. Shakespeare did. So why can't we?) There is a magical air in a house with a dog that has dogness in it. The magic is in the sounds—the sound of his tail beating on the floor because of happiness, the bark of a dog in play, his soft whine for love. The smell of a dog—well, it is a good smell, and that is part of dogness. And the dog lies around the house and gets in the way, and leaves hair that has to be vacuumed, and he makes messes when he's a pup, and all of that is dogness, but the dogness makes a house a home, and it brings a kind of joy to a home, a life to it and a wholeness that every home without a dog lacks. So we can say that without dogness, a house lacks something important. You can always sense it when you walk into a house without a dog. It seems empty even when it is filled with a lot of furniture and expensive things. I would rather live in a poor house that is rich with a dog, than in a rich house without one. You can quote me on that if you like.

Finally, you can quote me on this too: Dogs are the *double berries*. What I mean by that is this: Christmas is the berries. Birthdays are the berries. Catching a fish is the berries. But owning a dog and a dog owning you is the double berries. That makes a good conclusion for the argument.

So, to make a good argument, don't forget: Prepare, which includes talking to yourself and looking things up; find out what the other person wants or needs and aim your argument at it; quote an authority; tell a story; include some "heart stuff"; and end up with an unforgettable conclusion. Remember, successful arguments make successful living. So argue, and have fun, and get what you want—especially a dog.

G.S.

5

Keeping a Summer Journal

THE TIME of summer runs at a different pace and slows down so that you can keep up with it. Maybe it is because the days get longer up until the summer solstice.* After that we don't notice the minutes-a-day that days shorten, until autumn has sneaked up on us.

How many summers do a dad and son have? Important question, I'd say. Time may run at different paces, but it never stops. But what if, in the summer when time that has

---

* There are two solstices—December 22 and June 22, when where we are is either farthest or nearest to the sun's equator. December 22 in the Northern Hemisphere is the shortest day of the year, when we are farthest away from the sun's equator; June 22 is the longest. Just the opposite is true in the Southern Hemisphere. When winter is settling in, it is little comfort to know that it's summer somewhere else!

already slowed down, you could make it double over and stretch even more? That's what keeping a journal of the summer does.

A journal is sometimes like a log. Not a hewn tree, but a record. A log was where the captain of a sailing ship kept his records during an 18th-century excursion: "Log entry, July 17, 1789. Fresh breeze today from NNW. All sails set to run before the wind. No sighting of the Cape. Twenty-seven leagues. Fore'topman Bright confined below deck without food for sleeping during his watch. Water rationed. The Cape tomorrow or God save our souls."

A log is where Captain Kirk of the *Enterprise* enters his record of the day's activities using a star-date, not a date measured by the rotation of the Earth around a modest star called the Sun, which, in his memory, he has not seen: "We are twenty-two parsecs from the edge of the Andromeda galaxy traveling at warp speed...."

Keeping a log or journal of the summer is one way to stretch time. Just as in the logs of the past, on every one of your summer days something happens. Is it worth noting? Does it make you think of something that happened on another day— like the rings that expanded away from the first splash where you flipped the rock into the pond? If it does, does it teach you something? How does it make you feel? Is there something special to say about it? You can put all of this into a summer journal.

A journal can be a notebook, a sketchbook, a diary, or a memoir.*

A journal can also include drawings and diagrams, pasted photographs, and doodles that you did while waiting for your tetanus shot that you had to have because you were running around barefoot and stepped on a rusty nail. A summer journal can have paintings, maps and charts, weather observations and descriptions of the best fishing holes in the creek. A summer journal can record anything that you want. A summer journal can include your poems.

Your dad should keep a journal, too, though he may not have as much time as you have to keep one. But it will help him remember. And he will want to remember. He will not always have a son your age.

Keeping a journal is like doing something all over again— once when you do it, and again when you write about it, and then again when you read it later on. Time is turned back onto itself; summer becomes long enough for everything—even dreams. Especially dreams.

T.S.

*A memoir is a personal account of a time or an event; sometimes a memoir is the only way you can say what you really feel.

6

Finding a Hidden Treasure

ONE OF the most exciting things a boy and his dad can do together is go treasure hunting. Pirates always buried their treasure and had secret maps showing where it was hidden. The old pirates fought many wars over buried treasure. Sometimes in furious storms their ships sank with heavy boxes full of gold and jewels aboard. Today people dive deep into the oceans trying to recover treasure from these ships.

If you want to read a wonderful book about treasure hunting, read Robert Louis Stevenson's *Treasure Island.* It's at the library. It's about a boy—probably about your age—called young Jim Hawkins, who, with Doctor Livesey and Squire Trelawney, sets out to find a buried treasure according to the directions shown on a map that belonged to an old sailor. Oh, the adventure, the danger they go through! And do they finally find the treasure? You'll have to read the book. You and your dad can read it aloud, a little bit every night before you go to bed so you can learn all about pirates and buried treasure and other wonderfully exciting things.

You and your dad can have the same sort of fun right at home as Jim Hawkins had on Treasure Island. But first you have to have a treasure to bury. What will it be? A large can full of pennies, nickels, dimes and quarters? (One thing a box full of pennies reminds us of is that when we spend a dollar we are spending *a hundred pennies*. We ought not forget that.)

So what if Dad puts up the treasure? Why shouldn't he? He's the family exchequer,* isn't he? And here's how he can gather up our treasure: Every night when he comes home from work and empties his pants pockets, he can put the change he has accumulated during the day in a coffee can. In a few days or weeks he'll have put quite a surprising amount into that can, and one day the contents of the can—all of those nickels, dimes and quarters, and some pennies too—can become the treasure. Then your dad can hide the treasure and draw a map to help you find it.

Now, map reading is an important thing to learn. If we have a good map and we pay attention to where we are on the map, we can never get lost. And mapmaking is just as important. If the map is too easy, it won't be very hard to find the treasure and the

---

*Look this word up. Your family will get a laugh out of your calling Dad the family exchequer. Besides, a few words like this sprinkled in your speech here and there make people think you are very smart, which, of course, you are.

game will soon be over. If the map is too hard or not well drawn, we will never be able to find the treasure, and that's no fun either.

A good place to hide the treasure is in the woods where there are trees and old stumps and big rocks and paths and other objects that make good markers for the map. Maybe Dad will hide a series of maps, one leading to another and another and the last leading to the treasure. The map could direct you to go fifteen yards north on the trail that starts on the east side of the old cabin, or some such place. Which way is north? Which way is east? How do you know? Do we have to wait until it is dark and the sky is clear so we can locate the North Star? (I will show you how to find the North Star in one of these chapters. Look up the chapter in the table of contents.) Do we need a compass? You can get a cheap compass that will work just fine at one of the stores that sell auto accessories. Ask Dad which store. Do you want to spend your allowance on a compass? Can you find north if you know where the sun comes up in the summer or where it sets?

Maybe the map gives its distances in rods instead of in yards. Or maybe it gives its distance in meters. How much is a yard, a rod or a meter? You know, of course, where to find such answers. All of this important information is in the dictionary, that wonderful pal of ours that knows almost everything.

Now, the map could read like this: Start at the forks of Grey's River and Beacon Creek (or some such place). From there go so many yards or rods or feet or meters (whatever distance is chosen) north to, say, an old stump with a nail in it—

then so many yards west to a big granite rock. What does granite look like? Trees of different varieties can be used as markers. What is a hemlock? What about an old oak tree or a maple? Won't we have to learn something about trees in order to find the hidden treasure? And won't it be worth it? The trees will become our friends. Later on when we go into the woods, as we walk down a path and pass a certain tree we will be able say, "Hello there, Mr. Cottonwood," or "Good morning, Madam Spruce. Pretty green skirt you're wearing today."

Suppose your father makes the map, and after a while, maybe a day, maybe a whole weekend, you are finally able to find the treasure. Spending the money would be a lot of fun. But hiding the treasure again would be more fun. How about making your own map? Then see if Dad can find it.

If you can make a map to find a treasure, you can also make a different kind of map—a plan of how you are going to live your life, and the treasure at the end of the plan will be you. That's something to think about and talk about with Dad. There's more than one kind of hidden treasure. The real hidden treasure we all have is in ourselves. What riches do we have inside, down deep? What are our talents? These are our jewels. What can we do with our minds and our bodies? This is the gold each of us has.

So, go find your treasures, the ones you and your father hide out in the woods, and, of course, the ones that are hidden in yourself. It will take a lifetime to find those, but when you

find them you will not only be surprised, but you'll be made very rich by them, maybe not in money, but in something more valuable than money—you'll be made rich by *your own true self*. That is the real treasure you will surely find someday.

G.S.

7

How to Make a Beanie

ONE OF the most important things a fellow can look for is a perfect crotch, which is a perfect Y for a beanie which is another word for a kind of slingshot. I have spent an early lifetime looking for the perfect Y. Most trees do not grow perfect Ys. Or if you find one, it's way too large or too small. If it's a little too large, sometimes you can whittle it down to size so that each limb of the Y is about the size of your dad's ring finger. Besides being the right size, the perfect Y has to be of a wood that is very strong. I have never found a perfect Y in an evergreen tree. After you remove the bark, the skinned limbs of an evergreen are never quite strong enough, and they usually ooze pitch.

The perfect Y is a prize of prizes. You get so you are always looking up into chokecherry bushes along a creek bank to find the perfect Y, or in the elderberry bushes or other kinds of shrubs and bushes. And that is a good habit to get into, because if you get into the habit of looking into bushes you see a lot of things that other people don't see—like birds and birds' nests, and young magpies or jays that you can capture and inspect very gently and then release. It's quite nice to know that you had a bird in your hand and turned it loose and it grew up, so that when you are out in the woods and you see such a bird again, you know that you have been closer to that bird than almost everyone else in the world. And looking for the perfect Y gets a fellow in the habit of carrying along his pocketknife whenever he goes into the woods. The knife should be sharp. Have Dad show you how to sharpen a pocketknife on a whetstone.

If you and your dad are always looking for the perfect Y whenever you are in the woods and walking along a stream where the bushes grow that grow perfect Ys, and you finally find one, the slingshot you make will mean a lot more to you than one you might buy in a store. It seems almost like cheating to buy a slingshot, a cruel thing to do to yourself, because it deprives you of all of those wonderful searches, those outings to the woods when you could be looking, looking, looking for the perfect Y. One never wants to let some store cheat a fellow out of doing it himself if he can, because the pleasure is not in the buying, but in the making, in the doing.

Now, I'm not trying to tell you that you cannot find a perfect Y. Sometimes one limb of the Y is larger than the other, and but for that it is perfect. You can take care of that, of course, by whittling the larger limb down to the size of the smaller one if the large limb isn't so large that by the time you get it whittled down it's too weak to do its job.

Sometimes the perfect Y is way up in a tree. Those don't count because you'd probably have to cut off a large branch to get to the perfect Y, which is most often toward the end of the branch. And if you cut off the branch to get to the perfect Y, you might hurt the tree or hurt yourself climbing up too high without a safety rope. So I think you should limit your search for the perfect Y to bushes that usually are found growing near a stream or spring or in other moist places.

Now you have found the perfect Y! What a find! What a day! You could go ask your friends, "Did you find a perfect Y today?" and they will just look at you with blank looks on their faces. "What are you talking about?" they will ask. They will probably think you are very strange. And if you explain to them what a perfect Y is, they may or may not understand. But you don't care, because most of the things that are really important in this world, like finding a perfect Y, are things that other people do not understand. You and your dad know what a perfect Y is and how important it is. And that's enough.

Now let's very carefully whittle the bark off our Y and smooth the limbs down as best we can. If the wood is green, the naked limbs will feel cool and fresh in your hands. If the Y is from a dead limb, the limb will be harder to whittle, but you can whittle it smoother. You will see.

After you have taken off the bark, it's time to figure out what length to leave the limbs on the Y. Do you want short limbs or long ones? If you leave the limbs too long and hold the slingshot by the handle, you will soon discover that you don't have enough strength in your hand to hold it for a long pull. So my suggestion is that you cut the Y about like the Y on page 37. If you need to shorten it a little after you try it you can do that, but you can never make it longer. It would be terrible to find the perfect Y and then cut the limbs too short.

You can wrap the handle of the Y with string, and then glue the string and let the glue dry to make a very fancy slingshot. You can color the handle with some watercolors before you put the glue on if you want your slingshot to be really fancy. If you want, you can wrap the whole Y with string and paint it, and glue the whole Y and let it dry. Probably the string makes it stronger. But usually I was so eager to make my slingshot that I couldn't stand to do all the fancy wraps and then wait for the glue to dry overnight. I skipped those steps. I argued that the fancy slingshots didn't shoot any better than plain ones.

Now cut a notch around the ends of the Y the width of the rubber you are going to use. But before you do that, be sure you have the rubber on hand so you know how wide to cut the notch. When I was a boy we cut rubber from old tire inner tubes. Those are hard to find in these days of tubeless tires. But you can go to the drugstore and buy a couple of feet of surgical tubing, which is rubber hose about the thickness of a pencil. Won't cost much and it never breaks and never wears out, and it will work perfectly.

For the pouch to put the stone or bean in, go to the closet and get an old pair of worn out shoes—yours or your dad's—and use the leather of the soft leather tongue, or find some other leather that is soft and strong to make the pouch from. (Check with your mother first.) With scissors, cut the leather into a nice, even oval about the size of a hen's egg. Then at each end of the leather oval cut a slit slightly smaller than the diameter of the surgical hose.

Next, cut the surgical hose into equal lengths—about eleven inches for each side should be about right, because you are going to use up some hose length when you wrap it around each limb of the Y and some more when you fix the hose to the leather pouch. Attach the surgical tubing to the Y. You do this by having your dad loop the hose around each limb of the Y, one limb at a time, and then having him stretch out the loop as far as he can while you tie it as close as you can to the Y with dental floss. Go around the loop several times with the dental floss before you tie it off. Before you trim the floss, go around several times more and finally tie it off once again.

Do the same with the pouch end of the rubber, attaching the rubber to the leather in much the same way as you attached the rubber to the Y. Be sure after each length of hose is attached to the Y that each length is exactly the same. Otherwise you will be shooting all over the place. And remember, the shorter the rubber, the harder it will be to pull. On the other hand, if the hose is too long you won't be able to pull it out far enough to get the power you want. And when the rubber is too long it's hard to aim and shoot accurately. Experiment. You will find the right length for you. All boys' arms are not the same length and all boys don't have the same strength. The nice thing about what you are doing is that you can custom-make your slingshot.

You now have a slingshot, my friend.

But what do you really have in your hands? You have a weapon. And every weapon is dangerous. You can hurt people with it. You could kill a bird with it. I used to think blackbirds were bad because I didn't know any better, and sometimes I would shoot at them before I learned that blackbirds are beautiful, wonderful birds that should be admired and respected for their beauty and their strength. After all, they can fly from one end of the continent to the other, and they never hurt a thing.

You can shoot out windows with a slingshot. You can shoot out streetlights and do all kinds of bad things with it—just as you can with a gun. But remember, power and responsibility always go together. A slingshot gives you power to propel a rock farther and faster and more accurately than you can throw a rock by hand. With that greater power comes a greater responsibility.

Slingshots are great for target practice. You can set up a row of cans and get so good that you can hit all of them at ten feet away. Then you can practice shooting them at twenty feet. You can get so good with your slingshot that you can shoot it almost instinctively and hit whatever you aim at. Slingshots are made for use in the country, never in town, never at school, never anywhere that you can accidentally do harm with it.

Now, what you use for ammunition in your slingshot is very important. Rocks are the choice. You will get so you know the right size and shape to shoot, and you will get so that when you are out walking you will always be looking for such stones. Stones with sharp edges don't fit into the pouch well, create a resistance against the air when they are released and are not as accurate as rounded stones. The perfect stone is a perfectly round one, like a marble. So as you are hiking with your dad with your slingshot in your hip pocket, you can keep your eye out for stones the right size. Creek beds are the best place to look for stones. And looking for stones just naturally helps a person to be aware of other things along the trail and in creeks, so that pretty soon we become like the Native Americans used to be—we see everything there is to see around us, and that is quite wonderful.

By the way, if you practice enough, you will become a better shot than your dad. When you get good enough you can challenge him to a contest. Bet you can beat him after a while, unless, of course, he was an expert with a slingshot when he was a boy. Learning to use a slingshot is like learning to ride a bike. Once you learn it you never forget. Have fun. Be careful. And beat Dad.

G.S.

8

David's Slingshot

OF COURSE everyone knows how David slew Goliath. Goliath was a towering giant during biblical days. He came from Gath in Philistia and he represented the Philistines, who were at war with the Israelites. There Goliath stood, towering above all the men of both armies.

"Come on and try me," he hollered over at the army of the Israelites. "Let's settle this once and for all. I'll fight any man in your army, and whoever wins, wins the war." He laughed. "You are all cowards. None of you dare fight me," and he laughed again.

Goliath challenging the frightened Israelites was like a giant the size of a nose tackle on the Denver Broncos trying to bully somebody your size. No one could hope to fight Goliath.

Besides, he wore heavy armor all over his body and legs and had a sword as long as an ordinary man's spear.

But there was a young lad among the Israelites by the name of David who had no sword, no shield and no armor. He was a shepherd boy who had come to visit his brothers in the Israelite army and to bring them food. When he heard about Goliath and saw how the men in the army were afraid, he stepped forward and offered to fight Goliath. The king, Saul, turned the boy away, but the boy said he had fought bears and lions that had tried to kill his father's sheep and he had killed them all, and he said that Goliath would fall to him as well. Finally King Saul took off his own armor and put it on the boy, and gave the boy a sword. But David said no, he did not want such a nuisance, and took all of the armor off and laid the sword aside, leaving himself with only a simple slingshot for a weapon. And he took five smooth stones from the creek. Then he went out to meet Goliath.

When Goliath saw David coming, Goliath hollered with disdain, "Am I a dog that you come to me with nothing but a staff?" And he cursed the boy and said, "Come to me, you puny rack of bones. I will give your flesh to the vultures and the jackals." With that David ran toward Goliath, put a stone in his slingshot, swung the slingshot around his head faster and faster until it had great speed, and then, at the exact right time, he let the stone fly, which hit Goliath smack in the forehead and killed him. This is a very exciting story that you can read in the Bible if you want.*

But we are here to make a slingshot like the one David used. It's very easy. All you need is a couple of shoelaces, leather ones preferred, and a pouch made out of leather. Cut the pouch to about the size of a large apple. Trim a little leather off the top and bottom so that the pouch is longer than it is wide. Next, cut your shoestrings so that each is about eighteen inches long. Cut a slit at each end of the pouch large enough to thread the string through. Thread one end of the string through the slit in the pouch and tie it off with dental floss. (See Tom's drawing on page 45. The pouch looks exactly like the one on the beanie except it is larger.) Do the same for the other string, and you have David's slingshot—as simple as that.

Now you are ready to try your slingshot. At the end of one of the thongs make a loop that will fit snuggly around your third finger. Insert the stone in the pouch and hold both thongs tightly in your right hand. Swing the pouch around and around at your side, and when you think you have enough speed, release the thongs. The stone will hurl out at great speed. But where it hits is the problem.

Now listen: This is a very dangerous weapon. It is dangerous for two reasons. First, it takes a lot of practice before you

*You can read the story of David and Goliath in the Old Testament, I Samuel 17.

can be accurate with it. I never could get good enough with mine to hit the broad side of a barn. But David was very accurate with his because he practiced with it hour after hour, day after day, while he was herding his father's sheep. If you practice as much as David did you can probably get as good with your slingshot as he was. But if you are not accurate with it, it's like shooting a gun and you don't know where the bullet will hit—and that is very dangerous. Secondly, note that David could kill a bear and a lion and finally Goliath with his sling-shot. So you can see it is a lethal weapon. Therefore, you must go someplace where nothing is around that you can hurt with your slingshot—like out on the prairies or in the woods.

And even if you get as good with your slingshot as David was, you won't kill anybody or anything with it. Instead, if you're good enough, you'll knock the hornet's nest out of the top of the barn and run like the dickens. Or maybe you'll go float-ing down the river on a raft that you've built and shoot huge alligators and mammoth sharks and vicious bottom-feeding monsters, which, when you check them out closely, magically turn into floating logs and tree stumps along the bank. Or maybe you'll shoot Goliath, who turned into that big old cotton-wood tree down by the creek and all he does day after day is shelter little birds and make homes for squirrels, and who, despite his ferocious bragging and bullying, turned into a pretty nice guy after all. But be careful that the stone doesn't bounce back and hit you. Be quite a ways away before you shoot. You and Dad will figure out how far. Have fun. Be careful, and when you are walking, keep your eyes open for smooth stones the right size. I still look for them after all of these years. A smooth, round stone of the right size is always a great treasure.

G.S.

9

Hiding a Time Capsule

WHAT IS time? We get up in the morning and go to bed at night, and when we get up the next morning we say that a day has passed. A day is twenty-four hours of time, we say. But what is time? Or is that the right question? Does time exist?

Ask a tulip if time exists. The tulip says that time is a process that includes the sprouting of its bulb in the spring until the tulip makes new bulbs in the fall and then sleeps during the winter. Are you involved in the same process? Is your dad?

Some great minds have thought that time and space are somehow related. A fellow by the name of Albert Einstein thought about that a lot. But as for me, I think time is an endless river, and that we are on the river.

Whatever time is, we know that others will come after us. What would we like to tell them about ourselves, about our lives? What do you think is the most important thing that should be remembered about us when the process, whatever it is that we are caught up in, has been completed? Native Americans left us cave pictures, some of which are thousands of years old. Ancient people in Mexico and South America left us great monuments—pyramids, the remains of cities. Think of the pyramids in Egypt. Shakespeare left us his plays. Mark Twain left us *The Adventures of Huckleberry Finn*. So what would you like to leave behind to tell a future civilization about the most important thing that represents our time?

Suppose you have the power—and you do—to tell a future world about our world. You can put a letter in a plastic bottle, seal the lid and bury it. What do you want to tell them?

Let's think about this together: What would we say about the atomic bomb? Are we proud of it? Do we wish we hadn't invented it? Should we apologize for it? What will we say about computers and the Internet? What should we say about the human race? Have we become better or worse? Has our love for each other and the earth improved? Are we getting better at understanding each other and people who are different from us? Are we learning to take care of the earth? Should we apologize to some future boy who finds this time capsule for having hurt the earth, for having invented destructive devices like bombs, for having failed to put our knowledge to proper use, for having failed to outlaw war, for having failed to take care of the poor and hungry?

What should we brag about? We have discovered how to penetrate space. We can see into other universes. We have landed on the Moon. What else are you going to say about us that we should be proud about? And just as important: What are you going to say about yourself? What do you want a future boy to know about you? What have you done already with your life that you want him to know about and to remember you by?

Well, this is going to take some thought, isn't it? Maybe you will have to write this letter several times. Then, when you have completed it, and you are totally satisfied, you can put it in the plastic bottle, seal the bottle with silicon glue and bury it someplace that you know will be safe for a long time, a place where some boy in the future might be digging or looking, someplace where no one will disturb it in the meantime, like when someone comes in with a backhoe and digs a deep hole in the ground to make the foundation for a new house or building.

And when you have found the place and hidden your time capsule, as you go to sleep one night you can imagine how, many years later, a thousand years later, maybe two thousand, a boy your age is digging for worms or something, and he comes upon your bottle. What does this boy look like? What is he wearing? What does he do with his life? What games does he play? Can he travel to outer space? Or has he reverted to being a caveman? Does he care about his neighbors and the earth? Is he wiser than you? Does he fly around in spaceships? Does he have a summer home on another planet? Or does he live in a cave and hunt and fish with a stone-headed spear? Can he even read? What has happened to the human species? Maybe, after all, you will have something to do with who that future boy is.

G.S.

10

Flying Without Even Trying

WE ALREADY know that boys, and big boys who are their fathers, have always wanted to fly. I knew a boy who fixed up some cardboard wings, strapped them to his arms, and jumped off the garage and broke his leg. Everybody laughed at him and thought he was dumb. But I thought he was brave. Yet the line between bravery and stupidity is narrow. He just stepped over that line—and when he did he fell about fifteen feet and broke his femur bone, which is the big bone in the leg that attaches to the hip. After that we called him "Rooster," because roosters can fly, but not very well and not very far—but from my observations roosters always flew better than he did. I never met a rooster who broke his leg flying.

So when you are a mammal whose bones are too heavy and whose flesh is too massive to fly, which we are, all you can do is

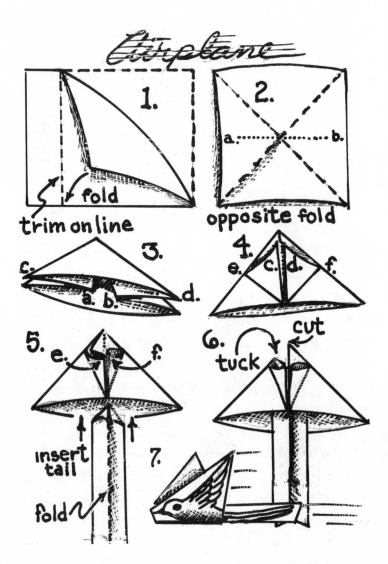

Airplane

1. fold

trim on line

2. a. .... b.

opposite fold

3. c. a. b. d.

4. e. c. d. f.

5. e. f.

insert tail

fold

6. cut

tuck

7.

to make flying machines. You can make a flying machine of paper, one you can throw out of the upstairs window and watch sail down to the ground so lovely and so proud. I used to make these wonderful paper airplanes when I was a boy. Then I would go to the pencil sharpener on a warm spring day when the teacher had the windows open, and when she wasn't watching I would toss the airplane out the window, and then at recess go down and pick it up again.

How do you make this magical plane? Start with an ordinary piece of 8½-by-11-inch paper, or you can even use a piece of newspaper cut to this size. The bottom edge should be the longest. Take the top right-hand corner and fold it over so that it lines up exactly with the bottom edge of the paper (see Tom's drawing, on the facing page, Figure 1). Now you can see that you have made a triangle. Cut off the left-hand margin of the paper so that you create a perfect square when you unfold the paper, as shown in Figure 2. Bring the folded corners together to make a new triangle. Once again, unfold the paper. The two folds have caused the square to be creased into four equal triangles.

Now comes the trick: Look at Figures 2 and 3. You can see that you are about to fold this square into a still smaller triangle with parts of the square folded in. This is actually very easy— just hard to explain.

What you want to do is pinch imaginery points (a) and (b)

(the center of the triangles on the left and right side of the paper) together, while flattening the top triangle to the bottom one. You can immediately see how you can manipulate the paper so that you end up with a triangle as shown in Figure 3. This triangle will become the airplane's wings. That move, like a lot of things in life, was easy, but it looked hard. Soon you will be able to do this very fast and the people watching you will marvel at your uncanny skill.

Next, take the corner of the top wing on the left (c) and fold it to the point. On the opposite side, take the corner of the top wing on the right (d) and fold it to the point. Now take (e) in Figure 4 and fold it exactly along the perpendicular center line of the triangle. Do the same for (f). See the drawing. Do you have it right?

We are ready to make the tail. The tail can be the same width as the paper you cut off of the top of the 8½-by-11-inch sheet when you made the original square—or slightly narrower. But this paper is a little too short when affixed to the plane to hold the nose of the plane up. As in making a kite, the length of the tail is critical—the right length gives the airplane the right angle of attack. I recommend you take another sheet of paper and cut a strip the width of the strip of paper you first cut off, but a couple of inches longer. It is always better to make the tail too long, because you can keep cutting off little pieces of the tail until the airplane flies exactly as you want it.

Fold the paper you have cut for the tail in the middle, as shown in the drawing, and fold in the corners at one end so that the tail is now pointed at one end, as shown in Figure 5. Next, insert the pointed end of the tail into the airplane wing as shown, so that the point of the tail fits into the point of the wing. From this point downward, with scissors cut along the center of both the wing and the tail that has been inserted, as shown. The cut should end where points (e) and (f), as folded, meet. See Figure 6. Tuck the two points into the pocket created at points (e) and (f), and press and firm up and fold the wings together so that when released they are tipped upward, as shown in Figure 7.

You can decorate your plane with colored pencils as you please. Make a bird as Tom did. Make whatever you please. Now you have an airplane—a first-class airplane that will fly better than any I have ever seen. It is actually shaped like the air force's B1 bombers. Everyone who sees your new plane will want one.

A little secret about flying it: Because of the folds, the plane is heavier at the nose than at the tail. If you turn the nose of the plane to you, and hold the plane between your forefinger on the top and your thumb and third finger on the bottom, you can throw the plane with a lot of velocity. Throw it the way you throw a baseball. Throw it tail first and as hard as you like or as easy as you please. The nose will come around just fine in the direction you have thrown it. It will fly differently at different velocities. If the tail wears out you can make another one. And with a little practice you can make an entire new plane in less than three minutes.

G.S.

11

Making a Summer Garden

A GARDEN is something that moves at the pace of summer. And like summer, it has to have spring to help bring it along. Spring is full of hope and excitement. The new warmth melts the ground's ice crystals and gives birth to the wondrous smells of damp earth and molding leaf and of the composting* of last year's garden.

Making a garden takes judgment, work, persistence and patience—and a place where the sun shines at least half of the day. And, as you'll soon discover, it's fun.

Judgment. You must use judgment when you decide on the size of your garden. One's judgment can be overwhelmed by

---

*Composting is the converting of last year's garden to fertilizer.

hope and excitement. Be careful you don't make a garden that's so large it either captures you or you leave it to neglect. If it captures you, you'll begin to resent it. If you leave it to neglect, you may feel guilty. Be modest with your first garden, perhaps make one ten by fifteen feet, something like that.

Match your garden with the things that grow well in your climate. Ask the folks at the greenhouse. Seed catalogs from mail-order seed companies like Burpee's and Gurney's describe where each of their products grow best and when to plant them. And maybe your dad knows as well. Speaking of judgment, it's amazing how few seeds and plants are needed to make a garden. You will almost always buy much more seed than needed, and you can't help it—a fact that is very satisfying to seed companies.

Work. You've now decided on the size of your garden and have a rough idea of what you're going to plant. And you want to get out into the soil. But first get some compost. It can come from the compost pile; it can be the lawn trimmings that "cooked" in the sun all last summer; it can be a pickup load of manure that you got for free because you offered to clean out a corral or chicken house. You can even haul it in the back of the family car in buckets from a local horse stable. I have friends in New York City who, in narrow planters, made gardens on their fire escapes. They traveled on the subways to the New York City Mounted Police Department stables and got buckets of the "good stuff" as they called it. I had another friend who, when he was just a boy, was sent by his grandmother early in the morning from Harlem to Madison Square Garden on the Broadway–7th Avenue Line when the circus was at the Garden. His grandmother instructed him that she wanted only elephant dung for her fire-escape planters. But we're not that choosy.

Spread whatever fertilizer you've obtained on top of your garden-to-be. Then get to work. But not when the soil is still too wet. Some say the classic test is to make a ball of the soil and drop it. If it breaks apart when it hits the ground, it is ready to work. If not, it is still too wet.

Using a shovel or spade, turn over the soil. Dig as deep as the shovel allows and work in rows, turning each shovelful onto the previous row. Work back and forth across your garden, like the plowman of old. A few things will become obvious: Even with gloves you'll probably start to get blisters, and your back will begin to ache. As someone said, "What a person needs for a garden is a cast-iron back with a hinge in it."

By turning the compost into the soil, you've enriched the soil by re-establishing missing nutrients—particularly the nitrogen-bearing compounds. Depending on your soil, you may also want to work in some lime, which is calcium carbonate, or gypsum, which is calcium sulfate. You can buy these minerals at the garden or hardware store. How do you know if you should use them?

Almost any soil will not be harmed by these two, given the quantities you will apply, and most soils are a little "sour"— particularly if they have been manured. So adding lime or gypsum can "sweeten" the soil, as the farmers say. And soils that tend toward clay, though good for growing, get tough and hard. Lime or gypsum will make them more porous. You can mix in the lime or gypsum by spreading it on top of your newly turned garden and working it in with a rake at the same time you break up the clods. Don't begin raking right away. Let the soil "breathe" and dry for a day or two. Otherwise you'll compact it with your feet. And you may be happy to give yourself a break anyway.

Now you're almost coasting. Plant your seeds according to the instructions on the seed packets. It may seem that the instructions have you making your rows too far apart and planting very shallow. But believe them! You can squeeze the spacing of rows a little bit, but crowding can make your plants compete too much for water, air and sunlight.

Here are some more things to think about:

Don't plant anything until you're pretty sure that it's not going to freeze again. Of course, nature can fool you. She likes to.

Early-producing plants that do well while it's still cool are radishes, lettuce and peas. Plant them first, and you'll harvest them first. If your yen to continue gardening extends into the middle of the summer, you can replant radishes and lettuce for a fall crop.

You can eat young peas shell and all.

Plant a few hills of potatoes, just for fun. You can cut some small potatoes into quarters for seed, but be sure that each quarter has an eye. The eye will sprout into the new potato plant. Plant them four to six inches deep. The frost won't get them. You won't harvest enough to last through the winter, but a dish or two of new shiny potatoes no bigger than Ping-Pong balls, smelling of the fresh earth and served in their pink skins and creamed with fresh peas, is hard to beat.

Pole beans save space because they climb. You can plant them on the edge of your garden. Let them climb the fence, or make a teepee arrangement of twine around a center stake and let them climb that. Beans love the sun.

As for root crops like radishes, carrots, turnips, beets and onions, if your soil is clayey, even with lime or gypsum, stir in an extra batch of grass clippings or leaves to keep the soil loose. The roots can't grow if they are pushing against hard soil. Plant root crops on an elevated row or ridge so they don't have to push against the rest of the garden to grow.

Be sure and plant a vine or two of pumpkin or squash. What plants! Their vines can grow as much as a foot a day. Their leaves, sometimes a foot across, are magnificent solar collectors on their hollow stalks—efficiency is the word—and when it rains, or you sprinkle the garden, the leaves collect the water and direct it to the base of the vine where often the plant is putting down auxiliary roots!*

Don't overdo the zucchini. These plants, as well as squash, will overwhelm you. Where I now live people cannot even give away their zucchini. If you leave your car unlocked—as almost everyone does in Wyoming—you're likely to find a box full of zucchini in the front seat, left there by the early morning zucchini commandos who skulk around before sunrise in the summer with boxes and sacks of zucchini to give away.

Sweet corn takes up a lot of space, but it's a wonderful plant. You need at least four rows so that the plants will pollinate properly, a job that the breeze usually does. Inside rows always produce better. Most varieties of corn produce only two ears per stock. Some gardeners plant corn in a spiral pattern in a circular plot to help pollination.

You can buy cabbage, broccoli and tomato sets at the nursery. Of course, you can grow your own by planting seeds in a window box on the sunny side of your house or apartment. Give cabbage, broccoli and tomatoes plenty of room. You can eat

---

*And by the way, if you want to make another kind of whistle, cut off a stem from a squash or pumpkin plant, trim off the leaf, and leave the large end of the stem open. Then just in front of where the leaf was trimmed, make a single slit about an inch long with your pocket knife. Compress the split stem against the roof of your mouth with your tongue as if you were playing an oboe. You have another kind of whistle.

young broccoli leaves as well as the flowers—which is the part you usually eat. Why does cabbage form a head? Why is some cabbage purple?*

To city-dwelling sons and dads: Some of the foregoing won't fit into your life. But I have known people who rented small plots of earth on the edge of the city so they could make a garden. It didn't cost much. Sometimes it was free; often it was gardened on shares.

On the Lower East Side of New York City, one of the most densely inhabited places on earth, community vegetable gardens have grown up where lots have become vacant from fire or neglect—particularly if the lot is on a corner where it can get sun. Balconies on high-rise apartments are productive; fire escapes also, though encumbering a fire escape is usually against the fire codes and ought not to be done.

Some plants will not produce without insects to pollinate them. Tomatoes, for example. In the city there are fewer bees, which are nature's most potent pollinators. In your balcony garden you may have to do their job with a Q-tip. Touching the stamen, the pollen-producing part of the flower, collect the pollen and with the pollen on the Q-tip, dust the pistil, the female part of the flower. Some plants, like a squash plant, have both male

*Any answer to these last two questions will probably be better than mine. Cabbage has a head because it's smarter than the other plants. Some cabbage is purple because it's more passionate than the green kind.

and female flowers. You won't do as good a job as a bee, but you'll father some fruit.

Persistence. After the garden is up, you must water it regularly if nature doesn't do it for you, and you must hoe or pull the weeds. Give your young plants a chance to get ahead. Keeping the earth loose around your plants helps them grow and encourages the rain or water from your hose to get to the roots. Water early or late in the day. It's more effective then.

Patience. Like boys, plants grow in their own time. Some grow fast, others slowly. But the summer is long enough for both. And you and Dad have many things to do together. While you launch into your other adventures, your garden is always growing. The harvest will be sweet and rewarding. There is something divine about gardening. As Francis Bacon, the English philosopher, said, "God Almighty first planted a garden. And indeed, it is the purest of human pleasures."

T.S.

12

Our Friends
the Grasshoppers

WHEN I was a boy grasshoppers were wonderful playmates. You can play "catch the grasshopper" and test how fast your reactions are. Are you fast enough to capture the little jumping beast before he gets away? He always dares you. He waits until you are almost on him and then, just as you are about to pounce, he jumps and flies away. Sometimes he will fly twenty feet or more. Sometimes he will hide in the grass and you can't see him. On a good warm day a full-grown grasshopper can make you sweat before you can ever catch him.

But suppose you do catch him. Now what? What do you have in your hand? Open up your fist carefully. If you hold him gently between your thumb and forefinger so as not to hurt him,

he will excrete a sort of tobacco juice out of his mouth and try to drop it on you. It is harmless stuff, but he thinks it will make you let him loose because it looks so nasty. Yet if you look at him carefully, despite this dirty habit, you will see he is quite a marvelous fellow.

There are many colors and kinds of grasshoppers, just as there are many birds and dogs of different shapes, sizes and colors. I have personally seen black-and-yellow grasshoppers, green ones, gray-and-olive ones, and some are nearly black. I have seen them with blue jumping legs and yellow jumping legs. I have seen them trimmed with red. Some have beautiful yellow wings that snap and click as they fly. And some are as big and as long as your father's thumb, and some as tiny as a housefly.

We can learn something from grasshoppers. They love to romp and play in the dry grass and fly from stem to stem in the hot sun. They are fun-loving creatures and never kill a thing or each other. Nor do they enslave each other like some humans do. They love their lives. Yet when the frost comes in the fall, and the other insects have found shelter in the bark of trees or have burrowed into the ground for warmth and protection, the jolly grasshopper may still be romping around, jumping here and there, laughing and playing and having a good old time, and then wake up one morning frozen to death.

I know people like that, and although I think that a person should spend his life playing (by that I mean he should spend his life doing work that makes him happy) we have to prepare for a time when we will have to face the frost in the fall. Ask your father what I mean by that. He will explain it.

And being a grasshopper is dangerous. They are standard food for hawks and other birds. Coyotes and foxes eat them.

They can hop into a creek or lake and become a feast for fish. Fishermen sometimes catch them and put them on hooks while they are still alive and throw them into the stream. There in the stream, in their terror and pain, they try to jump, and sometimes an old trout sees the poor bug, but not the hook, and likely as not the fisherman ends up with the trout in his basket for supper.*

Native Americans and other native people caught grasshoppers and ate them. I am told that even today a great delicacy in some places in the world is to dip grasshoppers in honey and roast them—something like eating honey-dipped peanuts. But I never ate a grasshopper. We do not eat our friends, do we?

These bugs have some marvelous attributes. They wear hard goggles over their eyes, which are made of many eyes—"compound eyes," the entomologists† like to say. They smell with their antennas. They hear with an organ on their front legs. How would you like to have your ears on your forearms and smell with sprouts growing out of your head and wear goggles all day every day? Maybe that wouldn't be so bad, especially if

---

* Yet in some ways grasshoppers are like humans. If there are too many of them they can do havoc to the earth. One year, six counties in northeastern Wyoming were declared disaster areas from an invasion of grasshoppers that ate everything in sight, and that year Tom lost his garden to them.

† An entomologist is someone who studies insects. I think one might safely say they have bugs on the brain.

you could jump as far as some grasshoppers jump in proportion to your size. If you could, you could jump in one great leap across the width of an average street, land on your feet, and think nothing of it. Just like that! Or you could land in a tree and not hurt yourself. So we should respect these little fellows for who they are and what they do and what they can teach us.

Now I'll tell you a secret. If you really want to catch a few grasshoppers to study, and they have outsmarted you during the day, you can go out at night with a flashlight and a glass jar with a lid. Go into the dry grass where they like to roost. You will find them hugging long stems of yellow clover or tall grasses. For some reason they do not jump at night, maybe because they don't have to be afraid of their enemies who only attack them in the daytime. Or maybe it's because they are afraid to jump or fly because they can't see where they are going to land. Whatever the reason, you can pick them right off their roosts and put them into your jar. Be sure to punch holes in the lid to let the air come in, because grasshoppers need oxygen just as we do. Put some grass in the jar so they will have something to eat, and sprinkle a few drops of water in the jar each morning. Now you can look at your visiting friends through the glass from bottom to top, and when you are through examining them and learning about them you can turn them loose. Do you know why we turn them loose? Because, if we love someone or something, the best way to show it is to make sure they stay free.

G.S.

13

Catching Butterflies
and How to Keep Them
by Setting Them Free

WHEN SPRING is solidly in place and the chilling echoes of winter are quieted, when the migrant birds reappear and the new green on the trees is moving toward full leaf, such is the time of butterflies. And with their fluttering and darting, their sipping at flowers and resting with pulsing wings, they will keep us company until hard frost. Catching and keeping a butterfly is part of summer.

You and Dad can make a butterfly net. A butterfly net is a tool, and like all simple tools it extends our body's abilities. The butterfly net with its willow branch or broomstick for a handle is an extension of your arm. You want it long enough, but not so long that you can't control the net. A little experimentation will point you in the right direction, but a handle length of about five feet seems about right for most people. To support the net itself, form a hoop using a wire coat hanger you've opened up. You can often find a good, old-fashioned coat hanger of nice thick wire in the back of a closet. The ends of the hoop that you make from the open coat hanger need to be bent so that three or four inches of each end, bent at a right angle, will rest on either side of the handle. Using about six wraps of soft wire, fix the ends of the loop to the handle. Twist the ends of the soft wire tight with pliers and cut them off. Bend the ends down flat. Finish off with a wrap of duct tape—that handy, silvery-colored stuff that's about two inches wide. Dad probably has these materials lying around the house somewhere.

For the net, use a piece of cheesecloth, which is a kind of gauze. You can find cheesecloth at a fabric store, or sometimes at the hardware store because it has many uses for wiping and polishing, or your mom might have some because people use it in cooking. Sew a two-foot-long, cone-shaped net, the base of which is slightly larger around than your wire loop. Roll the open end of the net around the wire loop, and using a needle and thread, sew the net to the loop. You're now ready to go after the elusive butterfly!

Butterflies are not as quick as birds, but the chances of scooping one out of the air isn't as easy as one might think.

You'll see. A butterfly rests often, landing on leaves or moving from flower to flower, sipping nectar. That's the best time to catch one. Reach out and cover the butterfly with the net. Then carefully lift the tip of the net up, creating an open cone into which the butterfly can now fly. Then, being careful not to injure the butterfly, use your hand to clamp off the net below the butterfly. This explains why a butterfly net needs to be long, with ample space. Now take a jar, such as a mayonnaise jar, and carefully slip it up into the net until you have trapped the butterfly. Remove the jar from the net with your hand over the top, and quickly put the jar lid on, one that you have first punctured in many places with a hammer and nail so that the butterfly can get air. Success! Butterflies have mesh wings covered with tiny scales that give them their color. If killed and mounted, they become fragile and brittle. A bump, even a brush, can turn them to powder. Besides, who wants to kill something so beautiful? You have netted a live butterfly, a piece and pattern of summer color. So how do you capture its beauty?

Watercolors are for out-of-doors and summer. They were the favorite of many great artists of the past, such as Paul Cezanne, John Sargent and Winslow Homer. Beatrix Potter illustrated the wonderful Peter Rabbit stories with them. Though they're simple, fast and not too messy, they're not necessarily easy. But you can quickly grow tired of easy things. Things that require practice to master and that can always teach us something new stay challenging for a lifetime. Watercolor painting is like that.

Keep your brushes clean in water, and mix your colors in the mixing compartments in the lid of your set, not in the paint pans. Using your watercolors and a fresh page in your summer journal you can capture your butterfly's beauty. Look at the butterfly carefully. Then, on the paper of your journal, lightly pencil in the butterfly's contours and the patterns on its wings. Observe the butterfly's body and legs, its antennas, and lightly pencil these in as well. Use a well-sharpened pencil with hardly any pressure. Then carefully mix and brush in the colors. You might do two or three views of the butterfly in your jar. You can learn a lot by looking at things from different angles, whether it's a butterfly in a jar or a problem you want to solve.

You may want to write something about the butterfly in the margins of the page: When and where you caught it, how, and what kind of a day it was. Or, if you have any thoughts about what it might be like to be a butterfly, nobody's going to laugh if you write them down. That's a good subject for a poem. This is *your* summer journal. You can write what you want!

Then it's time to turn the butterfly loose. Butterflies have things that they need to do and which they can't do trapped in a mayonnaise jar. But you've only delayed it for a little. It was a fair trade—the butterfly's time for its chance to become immortal in your journal.

One of the things the butterfly will do after you release it is to lay its eggs if it is a female. The eggs will hatch during the summer and turn into caterpillars. You can find these caterpillars crawling around on leaves and branches looking for a place to *pupate*, which means to go through a quiet period of transformation protected by a cocoon or outer case. If you put a caterpillar in your jar and include a few twigs and leaves from the site where you found it, it may form a cocoon attached to a leaf or twig, or to the side of the jar. Keep it in a cool, moist place, out of the direct light.

Although the cocoon appears to be lifeless, something secret is happening inside the cocoon. During the months that follow, the caterpillar is turning into another adult butterfly! When it is ready it will release itself by opening the cocoon, much as a chick pecks out of its egg. There's something to be learned from this. Sometimes the most important changes happen in secret until they are ready to be shown in all of their beauty.

Whenever the butterfly emerges, if there is summer left, release it and let it get back into the flow of its species. Some butterflies are migratory, and they will surely need to be on their way. But paint its portrait first. That's part of the bargain.

T.S.

14

Finding the North Star

WHEN SOMEBODY says to you, "You don't even know what's straight up," you will soon be able to prove to him that he is wrong.

"So where is north?" you can ask back. And the guy looks at you real strange and you say, "See, you don't know straight up."

Straight up on a map is north. But where is north? North is opposite south, but that doesn't help much either. There's a star in the sky that is, for our purposes, exactly, always, faithfully, forever, under every circumstance, good times or bad, in peace or in war always north, and that star, of course, is called the North Star.

The North Star also has another name that you might like to learn. It's other name is Polaris. Now that you know that fancier name you can, if you like, go around asking your friends if they have seen Polaris lately, and they'll likely think you're talking about your dog.

And you can say, "He's up there on the tail of Ursa Minor." That sounds like the dog is on the tail instead of the tail being on the dog. But Ursa Minor, which means Small Bear, is an old-time name for the Little Dipper. The North Star is the last star in the handle of the Little Dipper. For being the most important star in the sky it is not a very bright star. But you can see it, all right, and once you have it in mind—the last star on the tail of the Small Bear or Little Dipper—it will always be there for you. Always. I guarantee it.

Now, how do you find the Little Dipper? When people look up in the sky for the Little Dipper they often see a very small constellation up there that looks like a small dipper, but which is actually called the Pleiades, or the Seven Sisters. This small constellation is much brighter than the Little Dipper, which is made up of much fainter stars and is a much larger constellation than the Pleiades. You can find the Little Dipper by first finding the Big Dipper or, of course, Ursa Major, the Big Bear. That is the easiest, the brightest, maybe the largest constellation in the sky, and most anyone can point it out to you if you don't already know it. Go out with Dad and find the Big Dipper. See Tom's drawing on page 79. If you draw a line from star to star it will actually look like a big dipper up in the sky. I don't know how our ancestors got a bear out of it.

As Tom's drawing shows, if you follow the two pointer stars at the end of the cup on the Big Dipper, you'll find the last star on the tail of the Little Dipper—a faint star. And that is the North Star! Now you'll always know which way is straight up— at least on a map. You'll always be able to find north, at least on a clear night. And when you find the North Star, aim your eyes down from it to the ground. At our ranch, when I aim down from the North Star, a mountain called Castle Rock is right below it, so that in the daytime I can always see Castle Rock and I always know which way is north. You can aim down, too, at your home and always know where north is. And, of course, if we know which way is north, we also know all of the other directions.

So now you don't have to ask anyone which way is north. You'll have a friend up there in the sky that always tells you the truth. It has been a friend to sailors, who used it from the beginning of time to find their way around the world—at least in the Northern Hemisphere, which is everywhere north of the equator. If it hadn't been for the North Star—old Polaris—Columbus probably would never have discovered America, and none of us would know which way is straight up.

G.S.

15

Making a Bow and Arrow

IF YOU'RE going to be a young Indian wandering through the woods, you must know how to make a bow and arrow. You might come on to a huge old bull buffalo that wants to charge you or Indians from an enemy tribe who want to steal your ponies. You might have to fight off the white men who are trapping all of your beaver and mink and scaring away all your game animals as they trek with their wagon trains through your territory. Bows are pretty easy to make if you know what to make them of. And every Indian like you should have a bow and some arrows and be proficient* in their use.

---

*"Proficient" means skilled. An artist is proficient in the use of paints, for example. Use the word. Tell your dad that you have become proficient in asking for a raise in your allowance, if you have one—or something like that.

Now, where do we find the materials to make a good bow? The wood needs to have spring—a lot of spring—and should, after it is bent and released, snap sharply to its original position. Moreover, the wood ought not to get fatigued the way we get tired when we do an exercise over and over again. Different woods are like different boys. Some boys are stronger than others and it takes longer for them to show fatigue. The wood that is slow to fatigue is the kind we need for our bow. Otherwise as the wood fatigues, we'll never be able to predict where our arrow is going.

The pull of a bow is like the amount of powder that is put in a bullet. The makers of bullets put the same amount of powder in each bullet so that it fires exactly the same way every time. So it is with a bow. We want the arrow released with the same force every time. Now, what kinds of wood can we make such a bow from? In the East, hickory was often the choice of the Indians. But out West where I was born and grew up, we didn't have hickory. The best wood for bow making that my father and I could find was chokecherry. Oh, that wonderful chokecherry bush! As we have seen, we can make a whistle from it and it grows wonderful slingshot crotches. It can also make a bow or a fishing pole. And in the fall we can pick its berries, eat them, get our faces all dark red from the juice and besides that, bring the berries home to make jelly and jam. But right now we are making a bow, no?

Now, willow is also an acceptable wood, but it gets fatigued faster than chokecherry and it's not as strong. If you could find some osage orange or yew wood, these are the best of all. But they do not grow anywhere I have lived. Of course, you could go to the store and buy a piece of hickory or order a shaft of osage orange or yew from a source, but what's the point?

Half the fun is experimenting with the different woods in your area. When you see a nice straight limb about five feet long, cut it, take it home and let it dry until the limb without the bark is no longer cool to your hands and you feel that most of the moisture from the limb has left. Then, later, whittle on it until it takes the shape of the bow (see Tom's drawing, page 84). Ask around. Never hurts to ask a simple question like, "What's a good wood that grows around here that a fellow could make a bow of?" You never know what you'll learn if you just ask a question. Test the different woods. This may take quite some time. But you have a lot of time. Whenever you are in the woods, keep your eye open for a nice straight limb. Let it dry and whittle it into shape. Then test it. One day you will find the perfect limb from the right tree in your area, and then you'll be the expert on bow making. You can pass on the information to your friends and, one day, to your own son. The time it takes is worth it.

The arrows, of course, are the hardest of all to make, because we need arrows of the same length and, as nearly as possible, the same weight. They need to be straight and strong. The best arrows are made out of split straight cedar or fir. You can buy the shafts. I used to buy doweling at the lumber com-

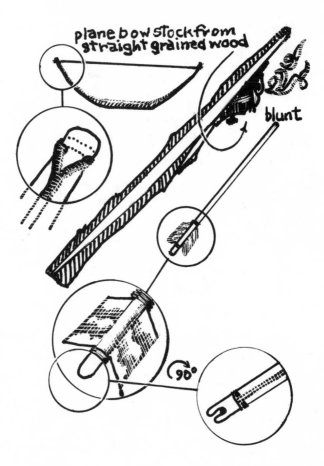

plane bow stock from
straight grained wood

blunt

90°

pany. It's hard to split cedar or fir boards into straight arrows. But if you select the right board, you can. Then you must whittle the split shaft round.

The length of the arrows depends upon how long your arm is. Make them a tad longer than necessary, because you will grow into them. It takes a long time to make a good arrow. Arrow making is something to do while you and your dad are stuck indoors by the fire during the winter. That's likely when the Indians made theirs. You can whittle while Dad reads you *The Adventures of Huckleberry Finn,* or you read to Dad while he whittles.

Carve a notch at the end of the arrow to hold the bowstring. This has to be done carefully or you will split the arrow.

Fletching the arrows is another skill in which you should become proficient. The feathers at the end of the arrow help the arrow travel straight and cause the arrow to revolve as it travels through the air. We need inch-wide feathers, all from the same turkey wing. Or you could use the wing feathers of other large birds. Chicken-wing feathers are not wide enough. My father and I used the wing feathers of a hawk we found dead one time. But you don't come upon dead hawks very often. The wing feathers of a peacock will also work. What about a guinea hen?

The arrows of modern archers are made with three plastic fletchings on each arrow. But we can get by with two made of feathers. The feathers need to be affixed to the shaft exactly opposite from each other, about an inch from the end of the arrow notch. You can split the feather stem so that it presents a flat surface that will rest against the shaft. And be sure, very sure, that you have affixed the feathers to the arrow so that the curve of each feather turns in the same direction, making the arrow spin in flight.

I used model airplane glue to attach my feathers to the

arrow because it dries fast and I could hold the feather in place with my fingers until it dried. (Sometimes my fingers stuck to the shaft as well.) The Indians used very thin threads of sinew and secured the feathers to the arrow with delicate wraps. You can use thread in the same way if you choose—or dental floss.

You need a weight at the arrow's tip end. Indians, of course, chipped arrowheads from pieces of flint. They would sit for hours on the top of a hill overlooking the valley below and chip away. I have found many a chipping on top of many a Wyoming hill where the Indians could see for miles. There they chipped at the flint while they watched the herds of buffalo below or kept on the lookout for their enemies, or perhaps they just enjoyed a spring afternoon in the sunshine. But we are not going to be able to chip an arrowhead. That takes a proficiency we don't have, which is to admit that the Indians knew things we don't. But then, we also know things the Indians didn't.

For the arrow point, we simply need weight at the end in order to hold it steady in its flight—not too much, not too little. Most of making a perfect bow and arrow is a matter of *doing*, which is how we learn almost everything in our lives—by *doing*, by trying this and then that. By experimenting, by getting into the wonderful action of doing something instead of just thinking about it or reading about it or watching somebody else do it. Let's always *do it!*

So let's experiment with what to put at the end of the arrow. We are not going to kill anybody or anything so it doesn't have to be sharp. You could get a small strip of lead and glue it to the tip. What other weights—it doesn't take much—can you attach to the arrowhead that will not be too heavy, just heavy enough, that will not cause too much wind resistance, and that finally will protect the end of the arrow from damage? Experiment.

We almost forgot the bowstring. The Indians used sinew. We don't know how or where to get sinew. So what will we use? You need a material that will not stretch. Nylon fishing cord won't do because it stretches. Cotton is too weak. So is hemp string. I made my bowstrings out of linen thread, a number of strands of it twisted together and melded together with beeswax. Linen is very strong. You can probably buy linen thread at a sewing shop or try the shoe repairman. He may be using a thread that will join together with beeswax.

Tie loops in both ends of the string. You can simply fold back the string four or five inches at each end and tie the folded ends into loops. Manufactured strings are looped at the end, the ends woven back into the string. Then the entire end of the string, including the woven part, is wrapped with linen. You can do this too if you like, but tying the loops as above is quicker and will work as well.

To string the bow: Begin by slipping the loops of the string over first one end of the bow and then the other so that the string is hanging loosely around the bow. Now secure one end of the string into the string notch at the foot end of the bow. With the foot end of the bow against the arch of your left foot, and with the top of the bow facing up, reach down to the grip with your left hand and pull the grip toward you while, with the right hand, you push the top loop of the string into the notch at the top of the bow. Now the bow is strung. When you are through using the bow, unstring it so that the wood doesn't fatigue.

By this time you have also made a quiver for your arrows and have a half dozen ready to go. Then off to the woods with you—off to the prairies, off to the fields. Be careful where you shoot. An arrow can go right through a person or put an eye out. Remember again: When you have power in your hands, you have responsibility for it. You will profit greatly if you learn that at the earliest age. Power and responsibility always go together.

But being responsible doesn't keep you from having fun. You can set up a couple of hay bales for targets and practice until you have shot all of those white men in the fanny who are standing in front of the hay bales—those white men who have been breaking their promises to you, who have been killing all of your buffalo and who are trying to run you on to reservations. You have to save your tribe. So get good with your bow. Get proficient.

G.S.

16

Damming the Creek

IN THE hot days of summer, when the moisture stored in snows in the high mountains has nearly been depleted, and pumps and irrigation for watering lawns and gardens have sucked the water from the streambed, and the creek has become merely a trickle that nourishes slack pools of watercress and algae-covered cattail bogs—that's the best time to dam the creek.

Damming the creek is not really stealing the water from things downstream; it is merely delaying it for a while, holding it in reserve to play with and to play in, and then turning it loose again. When I was a boy I couldn't help but dam a creek. Something in me made me want to do it. Could it be that I'm part beaver? Beavers have to dam up creeks, too. And I wouldn't be surprised if when you see a tricklet of water tumbling down, you, too, will look at that small creek and say to yourself, "I gotta dam that creek." So, if you are walking along one day and come upon a small stream, and if you feel as if you have to dam it, maybe you are part beaver. Or maybe we human beings are just dammers of creeks.

The first thing to consider is the best place to dam the creek. You need to choose a spot where the streambed is narrow and the sides are pretty steep. Otherwise, of course, it will require a wider dam. And since the dam should be made of materials available on the spot—rocks, sod and the like—a good supply should be nearby. Much of the rock will come from the streambed, and the sod can be cut from the bank with a shovel.

Once you've chosen your dam site, just like a real civil engineer, you might need to make a coffer dam above it. A coffer dam is merely one that will temporarily divert most of the water around the main dam site. You can build a coffer dam by creating a little bypass ditch which runs along and out of the streambed, at an easier grade than the streambed, until it is past your main dam site. The water will follow the ditch and dump into the creek below your main dam. You can then work on the main dam without having to work against the water. If your dad isn't helping you by now, go find him in the lawn chair and explain to him how a shovel works and that you need some help with some of the larger rocks. And when you get him down to the creek, a little splash of water to get him in the mood helps, too.

The dam needs to be wide at the bottom. As you stack up tier upon tier of rock and sod it can narrow down. You need an indent (a narrow, lower niche at the top of the dam) for the overflow, which will inevitably require a way to escape when the water rises to the top of the dam. Finally, when you are finished building the dam, you can disassemble the coffer dam, using the material for finishing touches on your main dam. Now your dam will begin to create a reservoir of water behind it.

When the water is high enough to run through the overflow trough, you'll have a pool behind your dam that is perfect to cool off in when the sun is hot. Perhaps it will be deep enough so that you can float on your back and watch the clouds. Maybe toy boats can navigate your lake. You may become the sea monster that rises from beneath the surface to snatch the people, or your hand may create the tidal wave that swamps them or pushes them high up on the shore.

And when we step back and look at our work are we proud of it? We changed the course of nature. That's what man has been doing from the beginning of time. He dams rivers and cuts roads and digs canals and irrigates the land. Man is like that. But sometimes man hurts the earth when he changes the course of nature. Already we have seen that our dam caused the water to rise and cover ground that never had water on it before. Perhaps it covered up some grasses and small flowers.

But one of the best things about being a boy and damming a creek is that we can un-dam it as easily. And so, before you go, let's turn it loose to run free and happy once more. You stopped it only long enough so that you could play together, you and the creek. And perhaps you will play again another day.

G.S. and T.S.

17

Kids* on a Raft

WATER MAKES a person ask a lot of questions: Where does it come from? Where is it going? How warm or cold? How deep? How swift? If you could ride its current to the end, what ocean would you join? What strange land would you see? Would you be welcome? Seeking answers, man took to the water in his first watercraft—the raft. And on rafts our ancestors first navigated the lakes and rivers and even crossed oceans.

Building a raft takes work on a hot summer afternoon. The first requirement is a ready supply of logs—not too big to handle and of a fairly uniform size, say eight inches in diameter and seven or eight feet long. A pile of wooden fence posts

*The biggest kid is your dad.

would be useful, or some dried logs from trees pushed over by the wind. Gotta have Dad and his saw. Together, you can find the logs and carry them to the pond's shore, where you can now begin to build this magnificent sailing vessel.

If you line up ten or a dozen logs side by side, you have the beginning of a raft. But you need a couple of cross members to secure each of the logs to. The cross members of course, when lashed, will hold the raft together. Tie each log to the cross members with rope—cheap clothesline rope will do—binding the log to the cross members in a crisscross pattern and knotting the rope. Then, without cutting the rope, move to the next log. This work is much easier done in shallow water—the water can help hold the logs up for you, and it's a good way to keep your feet cool. With this done, you have constructed the quintessential* raft.

If the logs are large enough, and have been dry enough— that is, if together they create enough buoyancy† your raft will support you and your dad on a maiden voyage. By means of a pole long enough to reach the bottom of a shallow pond, you

---

*Imagine what one of your pals will say when you observe very dryly, "You are the quintessential friend." He won't know whether you have insulted him or complimented him. He probably won't want to admit he doesn't know what the word means, so he might say back, "Well, I ain't a sissy, anyways," or something like that. So you'd better look up the word and know what it means.

†Take the time to look this word up. It applies not only to your raft, but to your spirit as well. Do you and your father have buoyant spirits out there building your first raft?

can navigate the pond by what is known as "polling," which is not what the politicians do to figure out how we are going to vote. But before the maiden voyage, the first question to ask is: Can you swim? If you can't, life jackets are in order. If you can, life jackets are still in order. Huck Finn, who was a very good

A view of the sail of the "square rigged" pond raft -the preferred craft of summer buccaneers.

YIELD OR ELSE

swimmer, would have worn one if he'd had one. He was a very smart hombre. And you still must take someone who can swim with you into the deep water, like your dad.

Back to your raft after its maiden voyage. You may want to add planking for a deck to make the raft easier to stand on.

Your raft may need some rigging—a mast and sail to push it slowly ahead of the breeze. A mast can be made from a thin sapling stuck into a hole in the center of the deck planking and then guyed—supported by ropes—to the four corners of the raft. A sail can be made of canvas tied to a spar—a cross-piece—near the top of the mast and guyed at the corners of the raft. Will you defiantly fly the Jolly Roger from the top of the mast? Will you beach on an unknown shore and bury your treasure of plunder by the light of the moon?

Or, anchored in the center of the pond, will your raft become fishing headquarters? An anchor can be made by filling a potato sack partly full of rocks and then tying the sack closed with your anchor rope, which is secured to a crosspiece of the raft. You can bring on board your willow rods, your hooks and bait, and begin to tempt a bluegill or perch to become your supper.

Finally, at the end of summer, the raft, like summer, must come to an end. The raft must be dismantled and the posts returned to the post pile, or the logs dragged from the water. If left in the water, the logs or posts will waterlog and sink, creating clutter in the pond, or they'll float off down the river and become part of the debris that spoils our waterways. Make sure your dad helps. Remind him: "When you're done with your play, put it away!"

Rafts can create wonderful memories. Next winter you'll remember the campfire you sat by at the edge of the pond while your raft rocked gently at its mooring. Perhaps you'll remember the stars you might have used to navigate by as the water slipped past the sides of your trusty craft and the breeze filled the sail. And you might remember the story your dad told you as the flames dropped and the embers of your campfire glowed orange: "Once upon a time, on a faraway shore...."

T.S.

18

The Unexpected Trip

AH, SWEET summer!

When school lets out, green becomes the theme, the sun is glorious and the days are long. With all the demands of summer—swimming, wading, fishing, exploring, climbing trees, building, serious playing, discovery, invention, loafing and dreaming—one of the most fun things is a trip that nobody, not even the one who pulls it off, expects.

Dad, let's say you work with a guy who is the friend of a fellow who knows a person who gets tickets for the triple-A farm team that plays in the larger town down the road—the Asbury Giants, for example. And this guy you work with never goes to the games and gives you the tickets. Perfect setup for an unexpected trip, I'd say.

You come home. You turn off the sprinkler. You cancel the

lawn mowing that you had set your son to in the morning even though you find it only half done. The dogs are sleeping under the lilac bushes. They can wait for their supper until you get home. Not answering any of his questions, you pile into the family car with your boy and then off to the ballpark!

By the time you've made the next to last turn and the big banks of lights that illuminate the field come into view, your boy has begun to figure it out. You park and find the gate. Then you go to the concession stand. Be a big spender—after all, a kid can only eat so much. Then you settle down for the game.

You'll see some players on their way up, and some on their way down, and some rehabilitating. Talk it up. Get into the game. Take time to look up into the sky and wonder if some other dad in the universe is as lucky as you are, watching some game somewhere with his boy.

It's going to get late. Don't begin to worry that you have to get up and get at it tomorrow. Stretch out. Summer is big enough for a surprise baseball game, or a drive-in movie, or a rodeo, or a county fair, or a night fishing trip on a party boat. That's one of the great things about time—it stretches. And that's one of the problems with time—when it's gone, it's gone.

On the way home you glance at your sleeping son sprawled out across the seat and still holding his Asbury Giants pennant. And then, when you look back into the tunnel of your headlights on the road, consider: Everyone will have something to remember, and when the day began no one had any idea what it would be.

T.S.

19

The Cave Dwellers

I HAVE never met a boy who didn't love a cave. That is because we are cavemen at heart. If you drew a line along a football field from one end of the field to the other, representing the length of time the human species has been around on this earth, the time we have been out of the cave—that is, the length of time we have been civilized—would be represented by something like ten or twelve inches along that total line. As a species we have not been out of the trees, out of the jungle, out of the cave very long. That's why boys all love caves.

Caves are the homes of our hearts. That's why we like dark rooms and candlelight. That's why we like to turn the lights down low at night and enjoy a fire in the fireplace. That's why people like log homes, because sometimes caves were lined with logs, and wood makes us feel comfortable and safe.

So we have to build a cave. And it will be more fun if we build it in a secret place. Maybe behind the garage in the backyard. But a lot better place would be in the woods where you and Dad can go on the weekends and take a lunch. Better bring along some gloves, because otherwise you are going to get blisters on those soft hands of yours from the digging.

We could dig a cave into the side of a bank, hollow it out and brace it with timbers, or we could dig a hole down into the ground and cover the top of it with timbers, roofing and dirt. There is only one problem in making a cave. We have to be as smart as the caveman. We have to make sure that our cave doesn't cave in on us, which could injure us badly. So we must rely on Dad to show us how to build our cave safely. But I will try to give you some tips.

Let's dig a cave on the flat because there is more flat ground around than banks to dig into. Let's be a coyote. A coyote doesn't dig out a den where everyone passes by. The coyote finds a secret place, a place no one is likely to come near. We are, in fact, entering the world of the coyote and the fox and the bear because we are, like them, digging our den—making our safe home. We are returning to the time when we were all animals living together on this earth in a better balance, which is a very nice thing to contemplate. *

---

* "Contemplate" is just a big word meaning to think about something. It is a useful word, however. You can say to your parent, "After contemplating the cost of an ice-cream cone I was wondering if you could lend me a dollar"—something like that.

How big a cave do we want? Well, first we have to decide who is going to be in this cave. Maybe just you and Dad. The bigger the cave, the more dirt you have to dig out, the longer and stronger the timbers have to be, the more roofing you have to put on and the more dirt you have to throw over the roof. So maybe you should make the cave just big enough for Dad and you. But one thing: It should be big enough for Dad to stretch out his full length, and it should be wide enough for the two of you to lie in side by side, and a little larger yet so you can store a few things there. With this thought in mind, maybe the cave should be about seven feet long or so and five feet wide.

And how deep should it be? A fellow wants it deep enough so he can sit up in it without hitting his head, and a little more. So have Dad sit down on the floor. Now tell him to sit up straight, and take a yardstick or a tape measure and see how much room your dad needs so that he won't bump his head when he's sitting. I judge that will be about four feet.

How many cubic feet of dirt do you think that you are going to have to dig out? How would you figure that? A cubic foot is a chunk of dirt one foot long by one foot wide by one foot high. So if you want to know how many of those squares of dirt you are going to dig from this hole to make your cave, just multiply seven feet by four feet by five feet and you get 140 cubic feet of dirt. Lotta dirt. Good thing Dad's along to help. You may have to spend several weekends digging this secret cave of yours. And what about the cream you rub into sore

DIGGING
A CAVE

muscles? Think you will need to have some of that handy to rub on your dad's arms and shoulders after a day's digging? Maybe yours?

Now that you have dug this hole in the ground and have piled up 140 cubic feet of dirt alongside the hole, what do we do? We need some timbers for the roof. They could be logs that you find in the woods. You could cut down some dead trees that are at least ten feet long, with a trunk at least six inches in diameter at the smallest end. You need at least three of these, which you will space across the width of the cave. Sometimes you can find dead trees that have fallen down that are still solid, and you can just pull them over to your cave and place

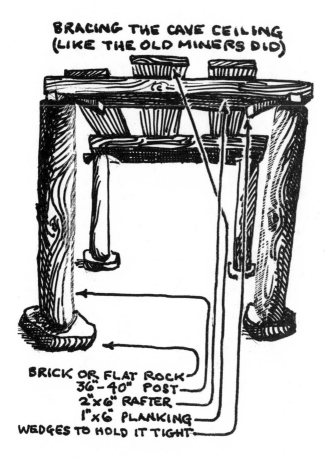

BRACING THE CAVE CEILING
(LIKE THE OLD MINERS DID)

BRICK OR FLAT ROCK
36"-40" POST
2"x6" RAFTER
1"x6" PLANKING
WEDGES TO HOLD IT TIGHT

the three of them across the width of the cave. That's probably what the cavemen did.

Next you need some roofing material. Cavemen probably used sticks and branches that they placed across the timbers. You can do that, too. They should be placed close enough together so that the dirt you pile over them won't fall through. Maybe you want to use old boards you found someplace. And maybe you want to put some tar paper or cardboard over the boards to keep the dirt from sifting into the cave. Use what materials are available to you. Our ancestors did. To keep the dirt from sifting in they likely used leaves or sod.

If you are near a creek, you can dampen the first layer of dirt into a mud of sorts and then pile the loose dirt over that. Don't try to put all of the dirt back on the roof. It will be too heavy and might cave in. But the roof should be strong enough to support a passerby who doesn't know there's a cave under his feet. Spread the rest of the dirt out a little, and pile leaves and branches over the remaining dirt and on the dirt roof so it looks natural. Remember, someday when you are finished with your cave you will have to fill the dirt back in. You dug it out, so it will be your responsibility to fill it in again.

But now, you ask, how do I get into this cave? You'll have to dig a little entryway down into it. And to be absolutely safe you probably should dig an exit, too. You can fix a piece of cloth to the roof so that the cloth hangs down over the entryway, making it nice and cozy inside. And inside you can dig out shelves from the side of the cave where you can store things.

Be sure never to build a fire in the cave. We have made no provision for the smoke of the fire, and to build a fire in this cave would be dangerous. If it is all right to build a campfire where your cave is, build it outside of the cave well away from the cave doors. Use a flashlight inside. Remember, the caves of cavemen were much larger, and if they built a fire they made holes in the roof or took other means by which to vent the smoke and make the cave safe. And one other thing: Ask your dad whether he thinks you need to shore up the sides of your cave for safety (I think you should), and whether the roof of the cave is strong enough for a large man to walk on without bursting the roof in. Making a cave creates dangers. Part of learning is recognizing dangers early on and discerning how to safeguard against them. Depend on your dad in this regard. Common sense will be your guide.

Well, now that you are a full-fledged caveman, go do what the cavemen did. Spend a night in your cave with Dad. Go walk through the woods that surround your cave. Learn about the other animals that share the woods with you. Identify the plants and flowers that are your neighbors. Learn how they talk to you as they bud and bloom and finally go to seed. Ask your dad to get you a flower book for your birthday. Learn about the herbs that grow in your forest. What roots can you safely eat? In your journal record what you learn and what you do. Buy yourself a bird book for your area and learn who the birds are, and what their songs are, and their habits. They will become your life-long friends so that whenever you walk though the woods you will be able to say, "Hello, Evening Thrush," "Hello, Mrs. Song Sparrow," and "How are you today, Mr. Jay?"

You will become so at home in the woods that soon life will

be so much better being in such a lovely place than in your room watching something artificial and silly on television, because in the woods you have the company of the real birds and real animals and real flowers. And the more you get to know them, the more you will learn to love them. It is a powerful feeling to become a caveman again, to be one with nature and to know that you belong on this beautiful earth.

G.S.

20

A Dandelion Necklace

DANDELIONS ARE the scourge of the lawn police. Dandelions are the target of herbicide* companies that sell chemicals to spray on the grass to kill the pesky things and make your grass green as paint and dangerous to wrestle in. Dandelions are the enemy.

But certain days of summer require dandelions. When you are looking for something green and tasty, and if your lawn hasn't been sprayed with herbicide, young dandelion leaves steamed and then salted and peppered, with a little butter dripping down through them, are a wonderful treat. Some old-timers used the blooms to make a fermented nectar called, of

*Herbicide is a chemical used to kill plants. Some herbicides are dangerous and can cause cancer and other maladies.

course, dandelion wine. And for a summer's celebration a boy ought to wear nothing less than a dandelion necklace.

For instance, you and your dad are out for a day of fishing on Dale Creek, let's say. You've driven as close as you can get, but that leaves about a one-mile walk down into the canyon. Since you're going to use a willow pole that you'll cut on the creek while your dad uses his trusty two-piecer, you get to carry the bag with the skillet and oil and boiled potatoes in it. Your canvas creel is dangling light and empty over your shoulder.

You arrive down in the canyon, it's a glorious day, the cotton-ball clouds drift from canyon wall to canyon wall above you and then disappear. The little stretches of meadow running down to the creekside willows are bright with dandelion blooms. But that's not what you have on your mind.

While you are cutting a willow for your fishing pole, you see the swirl of a nice trout lying in the shadow of the bank. You think you probably scared him, so you will let him rest and come back to tempt him later.

Your dad has headed downstream from the spot where you've left the bag with the skillet, oil and potatoes, and where you'll meet up later on. You rig your pole and begin to fish, using worms for bait first, the ones you dug last evening in the garden.

Your canvas creel is beginning to become heavy with brook trout so you turn back toward your rendezvous. When you get there your dad has already returned. He has cleaned his fish and left them in the cold water of the creek, strung on a willow stringer the end of which is under a rock so they won't drift off. He's pulled down the tops of his rubber boots and is napping under his hat with his head resting on one of his arms.

You crawl along the bank to where you can reach the place you saw the trout swirl while you were cutting your willow pole. The water moves slowly by, and all is quiet. You drop your worm into the small riffle that meanders toward the deep water along the grassy bank. You hold your breath. You are ready. The worm drifts past the spot where the fish was. Nothing. You try it again. Nothing again.

You stand up and call to your dad. He looks out from under his hat. He sits up and groans with pleasure. He throws you some matches and asks you to start a fire, and then offers to clean your fish. How can you lose?

As he opens his knife, he says to you that often the nice fish are overlooked because they are right in front of your eyes. "For instance," he says, "just as I was walking back I thought I'd look down along the bank about where you cut your pole. I sneaked up nice and slow from downstream and there, moving back and forth, was the nicest fish in the creek. I dropped a fly in front of him and bingo! When I got him into my hands I said to myself, "This fella has avoided mink and raccoons and king-fishers and herons all these years. Maybe even eagles." He gestures with his head toward the eagle nest high on the cliffs above. "Why should I mess up his run of luck? So I put him back. He took off downstream like a shot." Your dad looks at

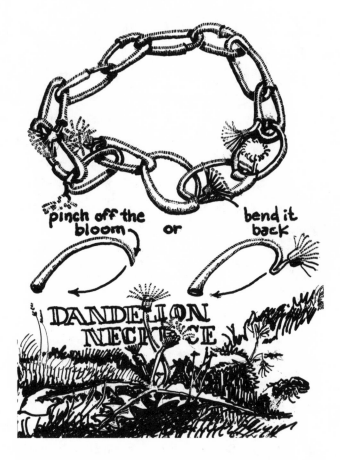

you to see if you get the meaning. You smile and add some dry
pine to the fire.

You eat your fill of fresh trout with fried potatoes. Your dad
had carried salt and pepper in his jacket pocket. The rest of
the fish are packed in your dad's creel to take home. You scour

the inside and outside of the skillet with dry grass before putting it back into the soot-stained bag. Your dad suggests another nap.

You wander out into the narrow meadow and begin to pick dandelions, leaving their stems long. You pinch off the less spectacular blooms from their stems and turn the hollow, tapering stem back on itself, inserting the small end into the cavity of the big end. It makes a link. You thread one link into another, bending the blooms back on some and inserting the bend into the cavity at the other end, leaving the bloom as part of the link. Soon you have a dandelion-festooned necklace. You put it on. You wonder how you look.

The cool and rocky ground wakes your dad as you are coming back. He looks up and notes that you have decorated yourself. You take off your necklace and he lowers his head so that you can place it around his neck. While he is making sure that the fire is well out, you fashion another necklace of dandelions.

You walk out of the canyon together, mostly silent, because the trail up is steep and breathing is more important than talking. As you approach the car your father does a little skip step and turns around, his arms in the air, his fishing rod in one hand. His dandelion necklace swings out above his creel. He is humming a tune, and now he's dancing.

He does not dance well, but he dances from the heart. You drop the bag with the skillet and raise your arms. You try to hum along but you don't know the tune. Ringed by your own dandelion necklace, you spin and dance until you are dizzy.

This leaves a question. Would this celebrated day have been possible without dandelions?

T.S.

21

Searching for Tinder

IF WE are going to be real Indians we need to find some tinder, because tinder is what we make fire with. It's that very fine, paper-thin, brownish bark from the underside of the bark of a tree that you can peel off and dry and which will catch a spark and magically, when you blow on it, turn to flame. There you have fire—just like the Indian. In our wanderings we are going to learn how to make fire by friction like the Indians used to do, and how to make fire with flint and steel as some people still do today, and in both cases we need tinder. So let's go find some.

Tinder in my country comes from beneath the bark—next to the growth wood—of the cottonwood tree. If you are walking through the woods down next to the creek where cotton-

Tinder from an old
cottonwood log.

woods like to grow, you will come upon an old tree that has fallen over like an old soldier. There it lies. In times past it sheltered birds in the summer—the robins and king birds and the little yellow warblers and the brown wrens and all their generations of babies. And it remembers how in the spring its leaves would be in bud, and how it would make clusters of green little pods that the boys like to pick and shoot at each other with rubber bands. And after that how the pods burst into cotton that blew from the tree out into the surrounding land like snow falling in the summer. The old tree lying there still remembers how in the fall its leaves turned all yellow and then came floating down and turned the ground golden. And the old tree lying there remembers the times when its barren branches were covered with snow as if someone had come along with a big bowl of whipped cream and coated every limb and every twig of the old tree, and the tree was proud, for it was the most magnificent tree in the forest. Then one day, like all living things, even the largest and the strongest and the most beautiful, it had grown so old and so large that it could no longer stand, and one fall a powerful wind came blowing down the valley to scatter the year's new seeds and down fell the old tree. There it lies, just as it fell, and you and your dad have found it.

Other trees in your area will create tinder as well. Evergreen trees do not usually make tinder, so you can skip them.

Look for fallen deciduous* trees. Discover which trees in your neck of the woods produce tinder.

If the tree has been lying there a long time, the bark will have become loose and you can pull if off, and on the underside you will find the strips of brown tinder, about the color of a brown paper bag with some chocolate streaks in it. The tinder is usually damp, even wet. Peel this off. Gather as much of it as you can carry home.

If you were native man you would find a large, high, dry, flat rock and leave the tinder there to dry in the sun. But we can shortcut that a little. Take the tinder home and lay it on a cookie sheet in the oven. Then turn the oven on low, turn the tinder from time to time and let it dry slowly in the oven. Keep your eye on what you are doing so you don't start a fire. The secret of good tinder is its dryness. It must be perfectly dry. You can't start a fire with moist tinder.

When your tinder is bone dry, pull it apart into thin shreds, the thinner the better. Now practice making a nest with it by cupping your hands around it and folding it and patting it. You will soon see that you can hollow out a small pocket in the nest where you can place the spark you will be making, as we shall

---

*A deciduous tree is one with broad leaves, like a cottonwood or a maple or oak. These trees loose their leaves every year. Conifers—trees like pines, spruces, firs and cedars—keep their leaves year round. Is the hair on the top of your dad's head deciduous or is it coniferous?

see in the next pages. With the spark nestled down in the very dry tinder, with small shreds of the tinder touching the spark, you will be able to hold the nest up above your mouth and gently blow upward into the nest until the tinder bursts into flames.

So now that we have our tinder, and it's dry, we're ready to learn how to make fire by flint and steel, and after that, fire by friction. You are ready to become the first boy of your generation in your town who has ever made such a fire. No one else your age in town will know how, unless he has read this book. But maybe the real reason you want to learn to make fire the way Native Americans did is because, in your heart, you are still an Indian.

G.S.

22

Making Fire
the Indian Way

PEOPLE STILL walk around on this earth, many with bare feet, who make fire with a piece of flint and a piece of steel. I saw tribal people in Nepal still lighting their cigarettes with fire sparked by flint and steel. They used a leaf for a cigarette paper, filled the leaf with tobacco and rolled it. Then they struck the steel at the end of their purselike necklace against a flint, saved the spark, blew it into flame and lit their cigarette. A lot of work to fill their lungs with smoke that will kill them one day. But we know better than that, don't we?

We want to make fire by flint and steel because we want to experience the excitement of making a fire the old-fashioned way—no matches, no lighter, no gas jets in the fireplace. If the world gets into trouble and we are in the middle of it, and we wake up one morning and no one around us has any matches and we want to build a fire, we'll know how. We'll just go out and find some flint and strike it with steel, and presto! Almost.

We've gathered the tinder already, don't forget. And we've dried it and stored it in a dry place. Now we need a piece of flint. Where do you find flint? The Indians were always asking the same question. They treasured their flint and chert* finds like gold. The making of flint weapons, spears, knives, scrapers and arrowheads was an early business of ancient man. If you walk through the mountains and prairies of Wyoming you'll find flint arrowheads and other tools and weapons and chippings nearly everywhere you look. Some natives traded flint for salt and for other valuables with distant tribes. And, of course, flint, when struck with a piece of steel on a sharp edge of the flint, will produce a bevy of sparks. Some flint, like some people, is more sparky than others.†

If you want to find flint in your area, find a geologist in the phone book. Or call the college or university near you and ask to be connected with the geology department. Tell the geologist

---

*Chert is a type of stone that resembles flint. It is made up of chalcedony, quartz, and silica.

†Before the Indians had steel, which came from Europe, they used certain iron-bearing rocks. The spark came from a minute piece of steel or iron burning momentarily in the air. What sets it to burn is the heat created by striking it against the flint.

I told you to call. Tell him or her that you would like to know where you might find some flint or agate or chert (quartz or quartzite also will work quite well)—that you want it to make a fire with flint and steel, and that you and your dad need to go out and hunt for some. I'll bet that geologist will be thrilled to get a call from you.

Or if you want to do it the easy way, which isn't nearly as much fun, go to one of the rock shows collectors hold around your area (or sometimes there are little rock shops on the edge of town), and the people there may know where to get some flint. Maybe, like the Indians, they will trade you a piece of flint for something you have. Find out. Tell them it is against Spence's rules to buy it. Can you think of any other way you might find out where flint or chert or agate can be found in your area? What about calling the closest United States Geological Survey office. Is there a state geologist in your state? Now is the time to become a flint detective.

Flint or chert can be found as individual stones out on the prairies and along the foothills of the mountains of Wyoming and Colorado. The stone is made up of extremely fine grains of quartz. It may look rather ordinary on the outside—even whitish. But if you break it, it will be of a different color on the inside, probably dark gray or brown or even blackish. If you want to know if it is flint, just break the stone and strike the stone with a piece of roughened steel. For the steel, my father took an old worn-out steel file and broke a piece off of the end of the file.* Your dad can help you find a short piece of steel. It doesn't need to be more than four or five inches long, and not too smooth, so that when it strikes the flint it makes sparks.

There is a trick to spark making. You'll discover it from practice. You don't just smack the flint with the steel. You strike down on it with a smart stroke, not too hard, striking against the sharp edges of the stone—the way a violinist sometimes strikes down on the strings with his bow. By practicing, you will learn the right stroke and the best places on the flint to strike. But how are we going to catch the sparks?

Catching sparks is easier by quite a bit than catching shooting stars. You catch the sparks in charred cloth. If you had a piece of charred cloth up in the highest reaches of the atmosphere you could probably catch a shooting star, too, which is nothing but a piece of burning rock heated up by the rock's entry into the atmosphere. You make charred cloth, of course, by burning it.

Find a piece of cotton cloth—not toweling, but simple cotton cloth, like off of the back of one of Dad's cotton shirts. Nylon won't do. Now go outside *with Dad* and find a place where nothing will catch fire. You and your dad must do this

---

*The advantage of a piece of file is that it is high carbon, which means that in the steel-making process carbon was integrated into the molten steel. This makes it very hard, so that it can be used to cut other metals, which is what a file can do. But it also makes a very hot spark for the same reason.

together and be careful not to catch yourselves on fire. Take a
piece of cotton cloth about the size of a washrag, and hold the
rag out from you on a long stick. Then one of you light the rag at
the bottom with a match and let it burn. Let it burn up completely. We want nothing left but the charred remains. These

totally charred remains are valuable because they will now catch your spark.*

Experiment a little. Spread an inch or two of charred cloth on the sidewalk or on the concrete in your basement, or in some other safe place. If the cloth has been properly charred, it will crumble at your touch. Make sure there is no breeze blowing. Now begin to strike the flint with your steel over the charred cloth, holding the flint as close to the charred cloth as you can while still being able to strike the flint. Eventually, to your surprise, you will see a spark catch on the charred cloth. Then quickly, carefully, lightly blow on the spark and you will see that it grows in size. When you can regularly catch a spark on your charred cloth you are ready to make your fire.

Next, pull out some tinder. Make a nest with it—one like a robin's nest. Cover the bottom of the nest with charred cloth about two inches in diameter. Put down the nest, with the charred cloth facing toward the open end of the nest. Then take up your flint and steel, and strike the flint until you have a spark caught on your charred cloth. Now carefully pick up the nest, tuck the spark into the nest so that there's tinder touching the spark, hold the nest slightly above the level of your mouth and blow lightly, but continuously, until the tinder bursts into

*The charred cloth has become a delicate, fuzzy network of carbon particles ready to do the job.

flames. There you have it! Be sure your dad is around when you do this, because you could catch yourself or others or something on fire. This is a good time for father and son to learn how to use fire safely.

So now you can do what the Indians did. How do you suppose the Indians made charred cloth when they didn't have any cloth? They used burned moss. You can try it too. How far should we go in becoming native man? As far as we want. We can learn things by going both forward and backward. We can learn how to make a rocket or how to make fire by flint and steel. I'll bet most rocket scientists don't know how to make fire except with a match. But you do.

G.S.

23

Fire by Friction, the Caveman Way

WHEN YOU are cold in the winter and you rub your hands together to get them warm, they warm themselves from friction. Friction makes heat. Friction can get so hot that it makes fire, and that is what we are about to do—make fire by friction.

Native man made fire by friction. He learned that if you rubbed two sticks together long enough, fast enough and hard enough, they would make fire. You can see him sitting in his cave or teepee, rubbing the sticks faster and faster, so that if he never made a fire he at least got hot himself trying to make fire. I expect that once he got a good fire going, he didn't want to let it go out, because making fire by rubbing two sticks together isn't the easiest thing to do.

spindle socket

(a dab of grease)

spindle →

leather thong

← bow

fire board

charred cloth and tinder

But in the same way that man invented the wheel, so he invented an easier way to get fire started by friction. He learned that if you make a bow with a string that is loose enough to go around a spindle, you can put one end of the spindle in a groove on a piece of wood, and play the bow back and forth like one plays the fiddle, faster and faster until the wood below gets so hot that it begins to smoke, and faster still until the wood itself catches fire.

Take a look at Tom's drawing above. You can make the bow out of a naturally bent limb. The leather thong is just a leather lace out of a boot tied to each end of the bow.* Tie it loose enough so that you can loop the spindle in it, but tight enough so that when the spindle is in place the string is fairly tight. The spindle is made of a round piece of wood about eight inches long whittled to about three quarters of an inch in diameter. Note how the spindle top is rounded. It should fit into the spindle socket easily. The socket is merely a piece of wood with a hole whittled in it so that the top of the spindle will fit into the hole and turn freely. Tom suggests that you put a dab of grease in it to make it turn easily. The Indians probably used bear grease or buffalo tallow. You can use any grease you can find around the house, including Vaseline.

The fire board must be made of extremely dry wood. If you can whittle it out of dried cottonwood bark an inch thick and three or four inches wide, that will be just right—especially if

* A leather strip about twice as wide as a bootlace is even better, because it has greater friction and will not slip around the spindle as easily, thereby turning the spindle better. You can make the strip hold onto the spindle even better by using some beeswax on the leather.

you have dried it in the oven in the same way that you have dried the tinder. Otherwise, any porous (non-resinous—no pine, fir, spruce or hemlock) dry wood will do. Cottonwood bark whittled into the shape of a board is perfect material.

Next, cut a bed to hold the bottom of the spindle. The bed is merely another hole whittled into the fire board to hold the bottom of the spindle so that the spindle will turn in this hole easily, but will also rub the sides of the bed as the spindle is turned—thus creating friction on both the sides and on the bottom of the bed. The bed should be cut near the edge of the fire board, as shown in the drawing, and a groove must be cut from the bottom of the bed to the bottom of the board so that the ember that is generated will fall onto the charred cloth below.

Now let's make a fire. In the bottom of the bed, sprinkle some finely ground, extremely dry wood dust. You can take a shortcut here in making wood dust by cutting a piece of very dry wood into the shape of a pencil and running it through the pencil sharpener. I suspect that native man didn't have many pencils or pencil sharpeners, and that he scraped the edges of dry wood to make the dust. You can do the same.

Fit the spindle into the bow as shown. Put the spindle socket over the spindle and get up over it so that your weight is bearing directly down on the spindle. Now, with your left hand on the spindle socket bearing down, begin to saw back and forth with the bow using long, fast, smooth strokes. The spindle will turn in the socket and, if you saw fast enough and hard enough and long enough, the wood dust in the bottom of the bed will begin to smoke and the dust will turn to an ember, which will fall down through the groove to the charred cloth below. As soon as this happens, carefully lift the spark up into the tinder nest just as you did when you made fire by flint and steel, nestle the spark down into the tinder and blow gently until the tinder erupts into flame.

This is not as easy as I have made it sound. It requires experimentation. That makes it fun. You'll want to experiment with different spindles and different woods for the fire board. Sometimes, for spindles, my dad and I used the large stems of native weeds that had dried over the winter. But a whittled spindle will do just fine. You will want to experiment with the depth and size of the bed, the kind of wood dust to sprinkle in it and the size of the groove. These are all variations that will affect how well your fire-making tools work together.

Don't give up. Remember, as a real man of the woods you must never give up. Pretend your life depends upon it out there in the wilderness. You have to make fire or eat your fish raw, and sushi hasn't been discovered yet. Besides that, a little fire in the winter will make you popular with the other natives who haven't yet figured out how to make fire. When you make it, they will paint a picture of "Fire Man" on a cave somewhere, and you'll become the "Cave Man of the Year."

Besides that, suppose one day you and your dad go on a fishing trip to Alaska. You are flying in one of those small planes. Now you hear the motor sputtering, and the pilot says, "Well, boys, we're gonna have to land this sucker somewhere." You are scared, but you keep cool. You see a small, barren gravel bar on an island in the middle of the river. You point. "Can you land it there?" you holler up to the pilot.

"Better try," he says. "Hold on."

By this time the plane's motor has died. You are going down. And before you know it, you feel the balloon tires on the Piper Cub hit the gravel bar and you feel the pilot apply the brakes, and there you are, safe and without a scratch.

You climb out of the plane and look around. You're a hundred miles from nowhere. The radio is out. What are you going to do?

You're going to be just fine. Your fishing poles are in the plane. All you need is a little fire. "Well," you say, "while you guys go fishing, I'll make us a fire." You use a lace from your boot for the thong. The rest of the material is there on the island—the wood, the tinder. But you may have to eat the salmon raw for a day or two while the sun dries out the tinder, the fire board and the wood dust. And if it rains, you may eat raw fish for quite a spell. Or Dad may just have a book of matches in his pocket, which, in the end, is the best way to make a fire on a river island in Alaska. So be sure to take some along in a waterproof container.

G.S.

24

Weaving a Basket

WHO WOVE the first baskets? Some birds, such as orioles, weave hanging nests; and robins twist grass, string and twigs into a bowl shape and then plaster the inside with mud, which they smooth with their own bodies. Certain spiders weave conical webs to trap their meals; some weave a sticky basket between their legs and drop it on their prey from above. The larvae of a certain species of caddis fly (which trout like to eat) make a basket in the underwater current to act as a sieve to collect food. People have been weaving baskets for many thousands of years—how long no one knows, because the material from which baskets are made, unlike clay or stone, does not often outlive the weaver of the basket.

One of my favorite basket sayings is, "Don't put all of your eggs in one basket." When I tripped on the doorsill of my grandfather's chicken house I found out soon enough what this saying means. Do you like scrambled eggs?

Baskets are marvelous things. They are mostly made of materials that in themselves are of little value—willow shoots, grasses, cattail leaves. Strands of these materials are joined and twisted, plaited and woven, until there is an inside and an outside to the basket. Baskets, of course, contain things. In a way, you can look at the world by dividing it up between those things you've chosen to put in your basket and everything else.

No summer is truly complete without making a few baskets. But what for? A basket, like almost every other summer thing, is its own best reason. Berry picking is always better with a basket, but a bucket will work as well. A collection of perfect pebbles picked from the gravel bar or beach is well stored in a basket, but the top drawer of the bureau will contain them, too. So mostly, making a basket needs no reason at all except that boys and dads need to make them.

Most baskets are round in shape, as a teacup is round. And for good reason. When you want to bend but not break something, you bend it into a curve, and when you want to get back to where you began, you travel in a circle.

Just like the first basket makers, you can find most of the materials for a basket alongside the creek or pond—willow shoots or chokecherry shoots, cattails or other reeds, certain sedge grasses, rye grass and the like. All of these natural materials will work, and, just as the robin does, you can combine them. Always be willing to experiment. That's what man is mostly about—experimenting and inventing things.

You and your dad can walk the creek and wade through the swamp on an excursion, looking for basket-weaving materials. Look for long, thin shapes that don't taper too much from one end to the other. Don't be in a hurry. There's lots to see, like blackbird nests and frogs, crawdads and salamanders, dragon-flies and snakes (most snakes are harmless little fellows who have to crawl on their bellies all of their lives, and therefore should be admired, not killed. Think what the view must be looking up from the ground when you're on your belly!).

When you get home, dry out the reeds and grasses in the sun for a few days. Later you can soak them to make them soft. You can do this with willows and chokecherries, too, though they can be used green. But they will shrink as they dry.

When you have your materials gathered and dried, make a little corral of stones in the creek and soak them there, or in a tub or bucket at home. You can even soak what you've gathered in the bathtub, but you'll have to remove it out before bedtime. It's not that easy to get out of taking a bath.

So let's make a basket. We are going to use *spokes* and *weavers*. Spokes are the radii of a circular beginning. That is a fancy way of saying that they are like the spokes on a bicycle wheel. Weavers are what fill up the spaces between the spokes by being woven under and over—around and around—under and over the spokes.

Take eight spokes, laying four over four to make a plus

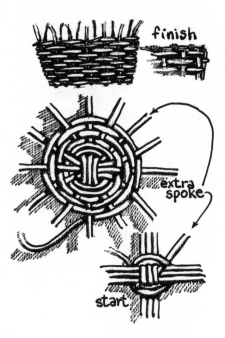

sign. Then take a weaver, which is usually thinner and more flexible than a spoke, and weave it under the horizontal four spokes and over the vertical spokes, circling four times, making it as tight as you can without breaking your material. This holds the center of the base of the basket together. Now begin to separate the spokes into pairs, trying to make the space in between each pair an equal eighth of a circle. This time with your weaver, weave over two spokes and under two until you've gone around once. Don't go around again because you'll be going under and over the same pairs. Something has to happen to make the "under and over" alternate, so that you go over where you went under, and under where you went over. This is the time for you to add an odd spoke.

Open up a little space where the first eight spokes cross, and poke an extra spoke in between the weaver and the first spokes. You can use a pencil or nail to help make that space. The odd spoke will stay when you have woven once around again. Sometimes you'll wish you had four hands. That's why you and your dad should be working together.

Now separate the pairs of spokes into single spokes, again trying to keep the space between each spoke even, and weave your weaver under and over each spoke. You'll see that with the odd spoke now in place, each cycle will begin as the opposite of the last—an "under" becoming an "over" and an "over" becoming an "under." And, you're off and weaving!

This is about the time that your first weaver runs out. Start a new one by overlapping it with the end of the old one, going back two spokes. And then away you go again. You can decide how many cycles you want to weave before you begin to bend the spokes upward from the base of your basket to form the sides. You can decide if you want a wide, flat basket—like the ones native people used to winnow,* the wild rice they col-

---

*Horses whinny. Natives winnowed wild rice, which is gathering it and then working the chaff away by treading on it and then tossing it up so that the wind blows away the chaff. Wind is good for winnowing. Oats, when winnowed, make horses whinny.

lected along the banks of lakes; or a tall, narrow one that might need a handle or strap to hang it by; or a bowl-shaped basket, great for fruit or picking strawberries or putting your spare change in, if you ever have any these days.

As you weave, bend the spokes up a little at a time. If you're going for a wide, flat basket you'll have to add spokes, because the space between each spoke gets larger and larger as you move away from where you began. To accomplish this, just poke a spoke into the space beside a spoke that is already part of your basket. If you add a new spoke beside each original spoke you'll end up with an even number of spokes again. So in one space you should leave out a spoke. Add spokes on the same side of each spoke—except for one space—and then weave new spokes in as you go around, shifting the spokes to make the spaces in between more or less even again. A couple of cycles, and you'll have the new spokes installed. You must keep your material moist and soft as you work.

Finally you'll have to finish off the basket. It's fun, but nothing can go on forever. There are lots of ways of doing this, but one thing must be accomplished: The last woven row must be "locked" to the spokes of the basket. Otherwise the basket will come apart. The easiest way to do this is to pinch (don't cut!) each spoke with a pair of pliers right next to the last woven row. Now you can bend a spoke at the pinched spot in the direction that your weaving was going—let's say clockwise—and use the spoke itself as a weaver. Weave clockwise over two, under two, and over two of the spokes. This will leave the bent and woven spoke inside the basket. Cut off the excess. Then take the next clockwise spoke, bend it and weave it similarly. As you work around the basket's edge, one spoke at a time, you will see that the spokes have created a rim on the basket that will not pull loose, and that the last row of the weaver is locked below the rim. Good job!

Dads are excellent for figuring out how this all works. Experimentation is essential. And when it comes to cleaning up, one of you can hold the dustpan while the other sweeps. And one other thing: Make sure that what you put in your basket is the right stuff. It's like life.

T.S.

25

Building a Box Trap

NOW, WHY would anyone want to catch some poor little hungry animal that comes snooping around, sniffing, looking, sniffing, looking, looking for something to eat? Although a lot of people eat animals, animals have to eat, too. I never knew a little animal that wasn't out looking for something to eat most of the time, and that's because they don't have a refrigerator or cupboard to store food in. If every time you were hungry you had to go outside and start looking around for something to eat, you, yourself, might be snooping under the porch or digging in the flower beds.

In the same way that we give human beings the benefit of the doubt before we condemn them, we ought to do the same for animals who make pests of themselves around our houses. I am thinking of squirrels who eat the bird food and gophers who make holes in the lawn looking for tender roots to eat. I am thinking of raccoons who come peering into our windows at night out of curiosity and who get into the garbage cans and make a mess. I am thinking of opossums who want to raid the dog food, and rats, oh, the ubiquitous* rats who, like humans, eat nearly anything.

So before we let someone poison these little animals or shoot them—a death sentence rendered against them for the small crime of looking for something to eat—we ought to find a better way to protect ourselves as well as them. Building a box trap is the answer.

Here is how the box trap works. Along comes Mr. Rat—Mr. R.P. Rat, to those who know him—looking for something to eat, and right there on the back porch is sitting this harmless-looking box. He follows his nose. His nose tells him there is a piece of cheese or bacon inside. But he can smell the smell of humans on the box, which makes him a little leery. His instincts tell him it is dangerous to go into strange places, and he does not remember seeing this box on the back porch before. Still, the smell of the cheese is just too much for him—like when we smell popcorn at the movies and we have to have a bag of it.

---

*Look this word up. It is a dandy. However, most adults who think they are very smart overuse it.

Anyway, Mr. R. P. Rat* cannot resist the smell of fresh cheese. It's too much for him. So into the box he sneaks. He runs in a step or two and then looks in front of him and behind him. He runs back out to make sure he isn't trapped. Now he goes in a little farther, and this time he can see the cheese just sitting there on the end of a stick, so tempting, so luscious. It all looks pretty harmless. So Mr. R. P. Rat creeps up on the cheese, worrying all the while that his cousin, Mr. Harold Rat, may be right behind him and grab the cheese before he does. Harold Rat is bigger and stronger than Mr. R. P. Rat. So Mr. R. P. Rat gets a little careless and at the last moment charges right in. He grabs hold of the cheese, but it won't come loose. Someone tied it to the stick. He gives the bait a good pull, and suddenly there is a terrible slam behind him. He turns to run out. But the way he came in is now blocked. A secret door has closed in on him. He is trapped!

Panicked, Mr. R. P. Rat runs from one end of the box to the other. He looks into every corner for an escape. He looks up and around and everywhere. He slams into the sides of the trap walls, but they do not give way. Finally he realizes that he is in very big trouble. And his nose got him into it. Damnable nose!

---

*What does the "R. P." in Mr. Rat's name stand for? You decide. But maybe it isn't Mr. R. P. Rat at all. Maybe it is Mr. T. G. Rat. Besides, who says that rats are rats? Maybe rats should be called guzzles or cheezits. Only people give names to things, and since you are a people, you can give whatever names to whatever things you want. Only trouble is, people may not understand you—which is their problem. Or is it yours?

Humans are the same way. Sometimes they get trapped into situations, into relationships or into jobs because they have followed something other than their good sense. Ask Dad to talk with you about this sometime. Anyway, Mr. Rat is trapped.

How can he escape? He notices this trap is made of wood, and he has good sharp teeth. He will gnaw a hole right though the side of the trap. So he begins to bite and chew at the wood. But we know that rats can cut holes though wood, so we will attend to our box trap before Mr. Rat can gnaw his way out. But what are we going to do with him now that we have him?

We are going to give him a new home—that's what. We are going to give him a free ride into the country. How many rats ever get to ride in an automobile? This rat is going to become a special rat. Someday Mr. R.P. Rat will be having his kids over for Christmas dinner and they will be gathered around eating sweet root pie and Mr. R.P. Rat will tell his kids how one time he rode in an automobile across town and into the country, and how when the automobile got to a place deep into the woods it stopped, and a boy and his father took the box he was trapped in, opened it up, and set him free in a new world. He had many adventures after that. He became a woods rat, and he was glad of that, he said. I have it on good authority that here is exactly what he said:

"I am so happy that I got transferred to the woods. I love it here because the sounds and the smells and the sights in the woods are simply swell. Before, when I lived in the city, I had to smell garbage and sewers and other nasty things. I smelled

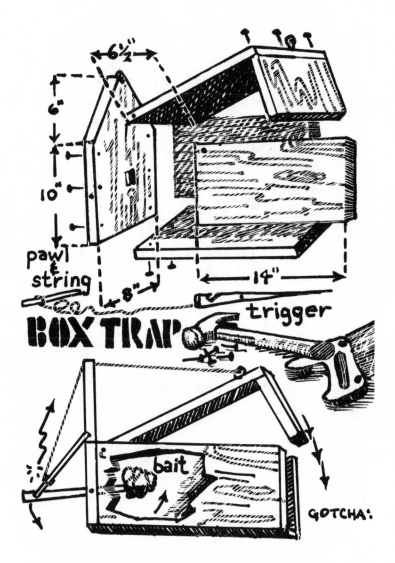

6½"

6"

10"

pawl & string

8"

14"

trigger

BOX TRAP

bait

GOTCHA!

them for so long that I didn't even know they smelled nasty. I wish I could find that boy and his father who brought me here. I would salute them."

So what do we learn from Mr. R. P. Rat's experience? We learn that the most frightful experiences we have to face sometimes lead us to new, exciting places. We learn that we can often rid ourselves of problems by being kind to those who cause them. We learn how to *empathize*. What do you think that means? We learn that we, too, are animals, in many ways similar to rats. Why do you think scientists use rats to do human experiments on? We learn that other animals have rights, and that our rights may be no more important than theirs in the larger scheme of things— that is to say, if we were to come back in another form and we could look down on the earth and see human beings, rats, deer, birds and other beasts in the same way that we look down and see ants, spiders, flies, butterflies and other bugs, we might not think humans were any more important than the other beasts we see. As a matter of fact, we might get very upset at seeing human beings destroying the whole of that beautiful planet while rats only cause damage in the backyard or in the basement. Be that as it may, we have caught this little pest and we have given him a better life in the forest because we caught him in our box trap.

How do we make a box trap? I think Tom's drawing above shows us how, better than words. Sometimes, as they say, a picture is worth a thousand words.

G.S.

26

A Mouse in the House

MAKING A mouse out of a cloth napkin is an essential art to a full life. If you know how to make a mouse out of a napkin, you can misbehave slightly at dinner while your parents are drinking their before-dinner libations, which, coincidentally, add about 30 percent to the cost of the meal and provide the waitress time to work on three more tables than she would otherwise be able to attend. I think you should recommend to your parents that they forgo the drinks and get right to the issue of eating. You're hungry.

A boy, if he knows how to make a mouse from a napkin, can not only entertain himself despite his terrible hunger, and thereby not become an immediate nuisance to his parents, but he also can entertain those at the table across from him. And this is important. Entertaining others is a talent that will serve him well throughout his life. Even in court I try to entertain the judge and the jury, not with a mouse made of a napkin, but with the same spirit of bringing some amusement to an otherwise dull experience. It is a good lawyer's job to occasionally say something light and funny—not disrespectful, of course, but something that touches the sense of humor we all carry with us to lighten the load of life. Children of all ages like entertainment, even the old ones such as the judge sitting up there on the bench, and so for a boy to learn to entertain others at an early age is important stuff.

If a boy learns how to make a mouse from a napkin, and how to make the mouse magically jump out of his hand, it will be noticed by everyone within sight. Your father will likely tell you to stop that. Behave! But one understands one's father. He is supposed to say that. It is his job as a good father to tell you to "stop that and behave," and it is equally your job, as the son, to push your luck—a little. A boy needs to learn when he must behave and when he ought to misbehave—just a little—in order to develop his independence, a sort of *rascality* with charm.

You smile at your father, even give him a little wink, and then you claim that the mouse, not you, refuses to behave, and to prove your point, the mouse jumps right out of your hand, and by now the people at the table across the way are cracking up, and even your father is laughing a little. Entertainment! To be a good speaker, a good salesman, in fact to be good at anything, one needs to know how to be entertaining—not always,

1.
START

2.
fold corner to corner

3.
fold triangle corners to center

4.
roll tightly

5.
finished roll

6.
fold ends to center

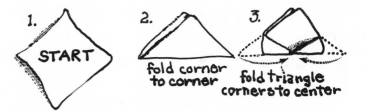

THIRTEEN STEPS TO A PERFECT...

BANDANA MOUSE

7.
pull tips back around and tuck

8. unroll this side as you roll this side

9. pull out ends

10.

11.
tail
pull ↑
pull ↓

12. twist
twist

13. tie an overhand knot

but at precisely the right time. So let's learn how to make a mouse and how to make it jump.

To make this *irascible** little fellow (as you can see from Tom's drawing above), you fold the napkin once so as to make a perfect triangle with the napkin, the folded base at the bottom nearest you. Fold the two ends to the center so that the ends just touch each other. What we have now is something the shape of a bishop's hat. Beginning at the bottom of the hat, start to roll the bottom of the hat toward the point of the hat. Roll it as tightly as you can. Roll until you get to a couple of inches of the tip.

Between your finger of the left hand and your finger of the right hand bring the two ends you have rolled together. You've made a circle. Hold the circle together with your left hand and unfold the tip of the bishop's hat, tightly wrapping the tip around the two ends you have been holding together. Continue to roll forward away from you and as you roll forward you will have to unroll from behind. Continue to roll forward and unroll from behind until you have come to the end. Behold! What you now have is a wiener with a tail sticking out each end. One end you leave as is to serve as the tail of the mouse. The other end will become the head of the mouse. If you spread out that end with your fingers it is shaped like a flame. Draw an imaginary line across the center of the flame. (Sounds complicated but it's

*Look it up so you can use it on the teacher tomorrow.

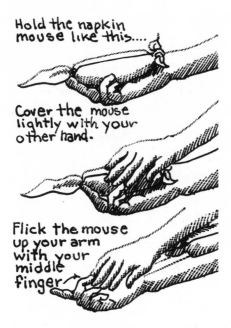

Hold the napkin mouse like this....

Cover the mouse lightly with your other hand.

Flick the mouse up your arm with your middle finger

going to be easy.) At the imaginary line you have drawn across the center of the flame, with your left thumb and forefinger grab the left end of the line and with your right thumb and forefinger grab the right end of the line. Now holding firmly, stretch the imaginary line as far as you can. You can twist the stretched material some and tie a simple overhand knot with the two ends you have stretched. (An overhand knot is the first knot you tie when you tie your shoe.) When you have tied this knot what appears is something that looks like a head with a couple of ears sticking out. What magic! You have just made a mouse's head.

Now the big secret. Open your right palm, palm upward. Take the mouse and rest his chest across the base of your thumb, with its back end at the tip of your index, or third, finger. Look at the drawing. Next, cover the mouse with your left hand so that whoever is watching cannot see your third finger, which will propel the mouse right out from under your left hand—just like that—as if the mouse were alive. Look, it jumped! (With a smart snap forward of your third finger you pushed the mouse out.) With fake desperation you try to catch it before it falls on the floor. Ah, you caught it. Now you put it back in the same position and pet it. Settle it down. Nice mousey. Be quiet mousey. Nice mousey. But no! There it goes again (you snapped it out again). And so it goes until you command the attention of the whole restaurant.

Your father looks embarrassed. But in truth, he is actually proud that his boy can command such attention with such style and charm.

And when you get into court and are faced with a dry old argument and a cranky judge, or when you sit at a meeting that has become insufferably boring, remember, you know how to entertain—just a little—not with a mouse made of a napkin, but with a humorous comment that relieves the tension and chases away the monotony.

G.S.

27

Fishing Side by Side with Dad

THERE IS a rhyme about Simple Simon who met a pieman going to the fair. In a book I read to my son, it shows Simple Simon fishing in a bucket of water, illustrating what a numb-skull this nursery-rhyme Simon was supposed to be. But fishing starts with Simple Simon's idea that there is a fish down there in the deep, cool, shady water—a vision. Like everything we do, it always begins with a vision.

Fishing takes time and cannot be hurried. And the best way to do it is with a friend—someone called Dad who is your best friend. But dads, like moms, are usually pretty busy. Most have to make a living, keep a home going and take care of many problems. Their list of things to do never seems to grow shorter. Sometimes our parents work too hard at it. And some-

times they worry too much. I'll bet your dad is no different. So you have to help him take an afternoon off or get home early from the shop.

Here's what I said to my father one time when I was a boy—and it worked.

Me: Dad, ya wanna go fishing?

Dad: Gotta work.

Me: We haven't had any trout for supper yet this summer.

Dad: Right. But I have to...

Me: (Interrupting—something a boy shouldn't do, but in this case I was saving my father from making a lame excuse and he was secretly grateful) I was digging beside the house and there's lots of worms.

Dad: Well, while I'm at work today and while you're diggin', why don't you turn over the garden where the radishes and peas were planted?

Me: (I have to keep my eye on my goal) I'll pick up a canful of worms while I do it.

Dad: If you get started early you can get most of it done before it gets too hot (I can see Dad is starting to come around).

Me: I heard that they were really hitting along the dam at Sutter Pond. Davy McStae hooked a hog. (The first part of this statement is probably true. Not too sure about the second, knowing Davy.)

Dad: (Rising from his chair at the breakfast table) Well, gotta get to work. (He pulls on his cap, which hangs on a hook by the door.) How big?

Me: Davy said the fish dove into the snags at the overflow. Snapped Davy's leader.

Dad: Make sure there's some mosquito dope in my fishing bag. (He holds the screen door in his hand. He has a little smile on his face as he looks over his shoulder.)

Me: Righto!

So the deal is struck. We both get what we really want, which is to go fishing. The bonus for my dad is that I've saved him from an afternoon of work, turned over part of the garden and stretched the walls of summer to include what I hope will be one of our several fishing trips.

To Dad: After you've found a way to take the afternoon off, leave it all at work—the worries, the pressures, the things you think you should be doing instead of fishing. There's nothing more important than a fishing trip with your boy. He'll grow up and have worries and pressures of his own. But if he can remember that one perfect fishing trip, he'll be able to hear his own son when he asks, "Wanna go fishing?" And don't forget: On the way home, pick up something at the store to snack on and a bag of ice to put in the cooler over the soda pop.

T.S.

28

Fishing with a Homemade Fly

TO FISH with an imitation fly that you can make yourself—what an idea! But it wasn't mine. Fathers and sons have been fishing with flies for centuries. Fishing with a fly is a different sort of fishing. When you're fishing with bait, you're dangling something in the water that a fish likes to eat. He eats it and you hook him. With a fly, you only want the fish to *try* to eat it. The challenge is to fool the fish, to be smarter than he is, and sometimes that takes quite a bit of doing. You want the fish to take the fly in his mouth for just that split second. Then whammo, you hook him!

Why would a fish try to eat a little bundle of feathers and thread? Because a fishing fly imitates something the fish likes to eat, such as an aquatic insect at one stage or another of its life cycle—though there are flies tied to imitate grasshoppers, minnows, frogs and mice. They're all called flies as long as they are made out of feathers, fluff, hair, fur, floss and thread. Sometimes chenille, beads, little thin rubber strands and tinsel are used to dress them up.

To make a fishing fly you need some simple tools and supplies: a vise to hold the hook while you make the fly, a spool of thin, black nylon thread, some thin wool or rabbit fur, some feathers, some clear fingernail polish, and, of course, a hook.

Feathers are available from many places. The most obvious place is a chicken yard. There is almost always a rooster running around. Hen feathers are not as good as roosters' for fly tying even though the hens think their feathers are fine. I have picked up feathers on the lawn, in the woods and on the street and brought them home to use for making fishing flies. These may be the most fun sources, because you never know if you'll find that feather again, and in your hands it may produce the best fly of all time. I often stop when I see a bird that has, lamentably, had a collision with a passing car and is lying on the edge of the road. I used to raise chickens just for the roosters' hackles. Most sporting goods stores have a fly-tying section where small "starter" packets of feathers and body material can be bought. Don't get carried away by the variety, remember the store is in business. Pick a package of nice mixed hackles, a package of yarn segments, a spool of thread. That's enough to get started.

You can purchase a fly-tying vice, but before you do, you should discover whether you want to tie flies as part of your fishing craft. To start with, you can make a vice with a simple pair of household pliers.

Here's how: Begin with a piece of one-by-four lumber about a foot long. With a pencil, mark the position of the ends of your pliers handles when they are closed (you will note that the distance between the handles widens as you open the jaws of the pliers). At each mark, drill two holes slightly larger than the thickness of the pliers' handles. Using a clamp, fix the piece of lumber to a tabletop. Put the curved part of the hook you are going to dress up as a fly into the jaws of the pliers and press the ends of the handles down into the holes that you drilled. This will clamp the jaws of the pliers tightly together and hold your hook so that you can work on it.

Now comes the fun—making a fly that will fool the fish! Follow along with the illustrations (see page 161). Take a few turns off of your spool of thread; put the end of the thread through the center of the spool. This will allow you to wind the thread on the hook, and the spool won't unroll as it hangs and keeps your thread taut. Starting at the beginning of the curve of the hook, wrap your thread around the hook in tight spirals three or four times. Then wrap backward over the first wraps. This will hold your thread in place. Your thread is now tied to your hook. Trim off the short end of the thread. Let the spool dangle while you select the material for the next step.

Most fishing flies have tails meant to resemble the tail or rear legs of an insect. Take a few feather strands and, holding

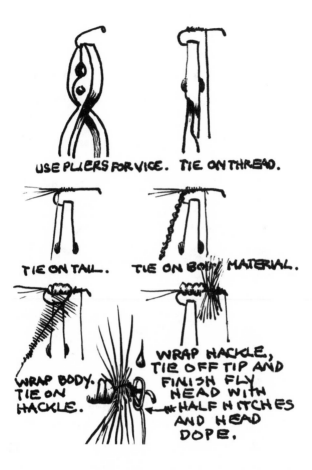

USE PLIERS FOR VICE.   TIE ON THREAD.

TIE ON TAIL.   TIE ON BODY MATERIAL.

WRAP BODY. TIE ON HACKLE.

WRAP HACKLE, TIE OFF TIP AND FINISH FLY HEAD WITH HALF HITCHES AND HEAD DOPE.

them in place where you tied on your thread, take two or three turns around the feathers with the thread. Let your spool dangle.

The body comes next. Bodies can be made of almost anything that can be wrapped around the hook. Let's try a piece of fine wool yarn. Tie on one end just as you tied on the tail. Carefully trim off the short stub sticking out. Wrap the thread toward the eye of the hook about halfway up the shank, which is the long straight portion of the hook. Let your spool dangle. Then wrap the wool in the same direction, wrapping each spiral snugly against the last, up to where the thread is. Tie the end of the yarn down with the thread and trim off the excess yarn. This is a basic body. But bodies on fishing flies are limited only by the tyer's knowledge of insects and his imagination. They can be striped, variegated, they can have tied-down backs, be bulged and fuzzy, or however you think you might like them if you were thinking like a fish.

What comes next? Some fishing flies have wings. Some don't. Some have wings tied upright and some wings are spread. These are usually dry flies that float on the water. Some have wings tied down over the back. These are usually wet flies, or flies that are fished under the surface of the water.

But many flies have no wings—just hackles. The word "hackle" refers to the neck feathers of a bird. Roosters, for instance, raise their hackles to puff up their necks when they are getting ready to fight. That's where the phrase, "getting your hackles up" comes from, meaning "getting angry." For fly tying, the neck feathers from roosters are usually used. There are also hackle-like feathers on either side and in front of the rooster's tail. These are called "saddle hackles."

To put hackles on a fly, take a neck or a saddle hackle by its tip and prepare it by carefully running it through your fingers to open and separate the individual feather fibers. Cut off the downy end of the feather and trim back a few fibers on either side of the shaft of the feather. Then, using three or four wraps of thread, tie that end of the feather to your hook just ahead of the body. Wrap the thread toward the front (eye) of the hook. Let your spool continue to dangle.

If your thread is getting short, carefully unwrap two or three turns from around the spool, work the thread through the center of the spool, and let it dangle again.

Take the end of the hackle and wrap it in the same direction as the thread. With each turn you will see that the individual fibers of the hackle will stick out away from the hook shaft. Three or four wraps of the hackle feather will be enough. Tie off the end of the hackle with the thread and trim off the rest of the feather. Be particularly careful not to cut the thread.

Wrap the thread around five or six times while pulling the hackle back out of the way with your fingers. Then make three half-hitches right behind the eye of the hook onto the wraps of thread. A half-hitch is a loop with a one-half twist that is put over the eye end of the hook so that the end of the thread is behind the loop. Pull each half-hitch tight. After the third half-hitch, put a small drop of clear fingernail polish—sometimes called "head dope"—on the knots. Insert a thin needle into the eye of the hook to clear the polish from it so your leader can pass through. Cut off the thread as close to the last half-hitch as you can. Remove the needle from the eye of the hook. Done!

No colors were mentioned here. That's part of the craft,

part of deciding what pattern of fly you want to make. At the stream or pond, observe the hatches. What do they look like? What shapes? What colors. Sometimes nature is wild with color, but not often with aquatic insects, particularly if the insect is in a larval stage or just emerging. Tans, browns, olive greens, beiges, blacks and greys are colors nature likes—and the colors that fish like, too.

Fly tying is a fine thing to do when you are preparing for that special fishing excursion. But how are you going to use the flies to fish with? Almost everyone has seen the classic arch of the fly rod in a fisherman's hand. A fellow can't fish this way without the right equipment, and there's certainly nothing wrong with having a good fly rod and a tapered line. But what if you don't have one?

All that a good rod and tapered line allow you to do is place a fly carefully in front of a fish without being so near to the fish that you scare it. You learn to reach out with your rod and line and leader. With your willow fishing pole you'll need to stalk your fish more carefully. This may mean polling your raft over by the weeds of the pond in the evening and staying still until the fish become accustomed to your presence, and then flipping your fly carefully near the ring where the last fish nipped at an insect resting on the water. Or it may mean getting down on your hands and knees, maybe even onto your belly, to sneak through the tall meadow grass so you can look down into a hole in the brook where the fish are cruising back and forth in the

slow current; and then raising your pole and flipping your fly into the riffle above the hole to let it float down toward the fish in a natural way.

Be ready! Like many moments in life, the preparation is most of the fun—and then whammo!

T.S.

29

Rigging a
Wild Fishing Pole

A FISHING pole and its rigging go together. Of course, you can spend all summer mowing lawns or delivering groceries so that you can buy an expensive fiberglass or graphite pole with all kinds of numbers and letters designating its "spine" and "speed," the weight of the line that should be used and the type and capacity of the reel. Such a pole will be light and lacquered, and it will break into sections with pretty wrapped guides, and it will come in a rod case. Your reel can have interchangeable spools that can be loaded with floating or sinking line, or woven or monofilament line.

A fishing pole like that is fine; a reel like that is magical; the different styles and types of lines all are exciting to survey—and expensive. The proper combination can be the right fishing pole for a lifetime. And having a job all summer is not a bad experience, either. It's good preparation for "grown up" life when you'll probably be working almost every day and will not have much time to go fishing.

But that's not what we're talking about here. We're talking about summer, those months of your life that are too few and gone too soon, but also when time slows down and opens up its possibilities. And we are talking about an almost primitive, elementary fishing pole—the pole that a young Izaak Walton* might have fashioned; the pole that Tom Sawyer and Huck Finn might have used along the big river of their adventures; the pole I used to catch my first trout with. Fishing doesn't need fancy equipment. Making do with a willow sapling cut from along the creekside has an appeal all of its own. You did it yourself!

Once you've cut your willow, or chokecherry, or alder rod, you need to rig it. You'll need some fishing line. It can be woven or braided or twisted. You can buy the least expensive spool of it. Or you can use some light cotton-orlon package-wrapping string such as the baker uses to tie a box of doughnuts closed. He'll give it to you. Or you may find it in a kitchen drawer. You might even "borrow" some from a casting reel in the bottom of a tackle box in the basement or garage. Ask first. Ten feet is more than enough.

---

* He was an English writer primarily known for *The Compleat Angler* (1653), which is a literary book on fishing.

FINDING A WILD
FISHING
POLE

Attach this line to your fishing-pole tip where there is a swell or bulge, so that once tied it won't pull off. Use an "improved clinch knot." You tie this knot by looping your line around the tip of the fishing pole and twisting your tying end around the rest of the line three or four times. Then thread your

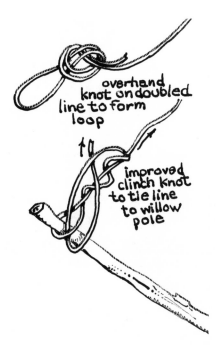

overhand
knot on doubled
line to form
loop

improved
clinch knot
to tie line
to willow
pole

tying end through the gap between the twists and the pole, and then thread the tying end back through the loop between the twists and the gap. Hold onto the rest of the line and pull the tying end. The knot will "clinch" around the end of your fishing pole. Sounds complicated. Look at the drawing above. It's easy once you've got the hang of it.

At the other end of your line, tie a loop. Double your line to form the loop and then, with the doubled line, tie a simple overhand knot and pull it tight. Trim off the excess. Now the line is ready to receive the leader.

Leader is a monofilament nylon cord. It is hard to see in the water. It is also usually smaller in diameter than your line. This helps disguise the fact that your hook and bait are attached to a line, which otherwise would look unnatural to a fish. Leader material comes in sizes and pound tests. Your leader should be somewhere around six- to eight-pound test. The pound test means that the manufacturer hung weights against the line and that the leader broke at the named weight. This does not guarantee that you can hoist a fish weighing that much out of the water, because knots and wear and tear will weaken your leader. The leader should be about thirty inches long when it is tied, so start with about thirty-six inches. Tie a loop in the end of the leader just as you did in the end of the line—double your leader to form a loop and then, with the doubled line, tie a simple overhand knot and pull it tight. Trim off the loose end.

Slip the loop in your line through the leader loop just enough to allow you to put the other end of your leader through the line loop. Pull your whole leader through and tighten the resulting knot, which will look like a square knot. If you are going to use a bobber, this is the time to thread your leader and line through the center of your cork bobber (see Chapter 30, "Finding the Fish—Making a Bobber"). Fix it on the line. You can adjust your bait depth later.

At the other end of the leader you can tie a hook using an "improved clinch knot"—remember that one? Or, if your hooks are snelled, which means when you buy them they already have a short leader tied onto them with a loop in the end, you will tie

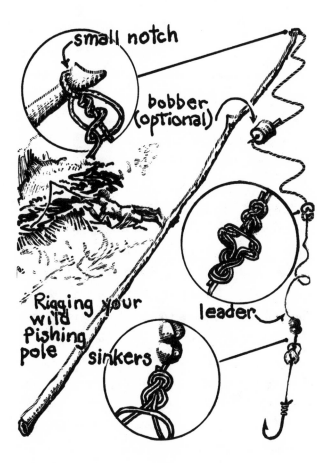

small notch

bobber
(optional)

Rigging your
wild
Fishing
pole

leader

sinkers

a loop in that end of the leader and attach the hook the same way that you attached the line to the leader.

Finally, if you are going to bait fish, you'll need to attach sinkers to your leader about eight to ten inches above the hook. If they are too close to your hook, your bait will not move naturally in the water. Use split-shot sinkers made from lead. Split shot comes in many sizes. Try a medium size. Pinch on two of them nice and tight with pliers (you shouldn't use your teeth, but if you do, bite slowly, easily until the split shot is tightly closed so the sinkers don't slide).

Now you're ready for some bait. What'll it be? Worm, grasshopper, doughball, a chunk of cheese? Here's where the type of fish you're after, local conditions, listening to one of the old-timers, experimentation and whimsy* come into play. I knew a fellow named Jake. He claimed he always put a little wad of cheese on his hook along with an earthworm. He said the smell of the two together in the water drove the fish "plumb crazy." Jake used a willow pole rigged in much the way I have described above. He fished off of a cut bank near the inlet of an irrigation lake. Jake was the master of the blue gill. And who could argue with him? He always brought home a bagful. But when I tried his bait combo, it didn't seem to make any difference. I wouldn't be surprised if he used a secret bait. I have a secret combination of my own, and you'll find yours. That, in part, is what fishing is about.

T.S.

---

* "Whimsy" really means whatever seems to suit your fancy. I mean, you may like striped underwear rather than polka dot, or you may want to wear polka dot underwear on Wednesday and striped underwear on Sunday, all of which is a matter of whimsy.

30

Finding the Fish—
Making a Bobber

A BOBBER can serve a number of purposes while you're fishing in still waters, such as a pond or a large, deep hole in a river. You may not be able to see down into the water because it's murky or deep. So you watch your bobber, and your bobber tells you what's going on down there. When it bobs, the fish is mouthing your bait; when it goes below the surface you have a bite, because the fish is running with it, and that pulls the bobber down.

Another purpose a bobber serves is to keep your bait at a proper level in the water. Fish go where the food is, and from day to day that can be at different levels. And different species of fish may not share the same levels in the same water. Catfish and carp, for example, are mostly bottom feeders. Their mouths are positioned on the undersides of their heads, as if their mouths were under their chins. A carp has a small mouth. A catfish has a very large one. That tells you that a catfish is capable of gulping a large piece of food from the bottom, but a carp can only take in small bits and scraps. Neither of them has teeth.

Crappies and perch, rock bass and bluegills cruise around and eat wherever they can find food. So if your bait is resting at a level where they aren't, you won't have much luck. Trout, bass, pickerel, pike and walleyes also feed at any level.

Where are the fish today? Finding them doesn't have to be an utterly hit-and-miss proposition. Having an idea of where to look is part of fishing. And once you've found the level, a bobber can keep your bait at that "sweet spot," and a good supper is a little closer to the creel.

But how do you find that level? Fish don't often swim where they'll be in danger of becoming a meal for a heron, eagle, or kingfisher, unless they're small, newly hatched minnows hiding in weeds and snags in the shallows near the spot where they were born.

Fish don't often inhabit waters that are uncomfortable. Water that's too warm has a reduced oxygen content, which is unpleasant for the fish. Warm water is also usually shallow water, which is dangerous. But sometimes, such as during a rain storm, more oxygen will be dissolved into the water by the splashing of the raindrops on the water's surface, which might bring fish closer to the surface.

Fish, like all animals, would rather conserve energy, so they won't be found in the swiftest currents unless they are going somewhere or unless they're tucked away in a small eddy, enjoying the greater amount of oxygen that's being stirred into the tumbling water. At the edge of a current where there's a swirl and the water slows down, a fish can rest and at the same time watch for food that the current may be bringing. That's a spot where a fish just might be hanging around. But a bobber won't do you much good in this kind of water.

Water in the shade, where there's a cut bank or overhanging grass or bushes that offer cover and a cool layer of water—that's a spot to consider. The edges of waterweed patches, where you can see the tips of the weeds on the surface, is another good spot to find a lolling fish. All kinds of underwater life, such as underwater beetles, insect larvae, tadpoles and frogs hang around waterweeds, and that may be where the fish are feeding.

Of course, during the summer the deepest part of the pond or fishing hole is usually the coolest, and the fish will often seek that comfort, so fishing near the bottom on a hot day is a pretty good idea to start with—but not right on the bottom where your bait can sink into the ooze or get lost behind a rock. And at the bottom there is often a layer of decaying plant matter that gives off gasses that reduce the oxygen in the water. That's a bad place for a fish to wander into. So a bobber can keep your bait up off the bottom and present it to the fish in the best way.

If it is too cool down there—because there's an ice-cold underwater spring, for instance—then insect larvae and other living things won't be hatching, and consequently there won't be much there for a fish to eat. That's when a bobber can keep your bait on the upper edge of the cool level where the fish will be hanging out.

If there's a slow current in a river it can drift your bait. That's not a bad thing. True, you must reposition your bait after it's drifted through the area where you think the fish are. On the other hand, if you want to keep your bait in a special spot in a hole, you can rig your line with a sinker heavy enough to hold the bottom with your hook above it a foot or so, and then your bobber farther up the line.

That's what your bobber is for—telling you about things you can't see and helping you keep your bait in places you only have a mental picture of. It's a fine skill to develop—being able to visualize what a place looks like that you've never seen, and then planning to reach into it with your tools, which are your fishing pole and line, your hook, your sinker and your bobber. And having your plan bear fruit, or in this case, fish—that is nearly divine.

A plastic bobber can be bought, but why? Often we hurry to get to the goal, only to realize that we've missed most of the fun. So how about making a bobber?

You can begin with a cork made out of natural cork bark, one out of a bottle or from a collection of corks of various sizes that come in packages at the hardware store. Cork is good because it is very light and buoyant. Using a drill, drill a hole through the center. Trim down a stick so that it is tapered and slightly larger at its wide end than the hole in the cork. Your fishing line must pass through the hole before you tie on your hook. You decide how far up the line you want your bobber, and hold it there by pushing the tapered stick carefully into the hole until it's snug. Such is the classic bobber.

But you can make it fancier. You can round it by sanding it on medium sandpaper into a spherical or oval shape; you can paint it with model airplane paint, giving it your special color and pattern signature. It's a fun thing to do with your dad the night before you head to the pond with him. And, if you catch more fish than he does, you can boast that it was that special paint job on your bobber that made the difference.

When you've helped clean the fish and stood by the skillet while the fish are being turned in the light oil as they cook, and when the fish are hot and tender and flaky on the supper table, you can plead that the extra effort of catching more fish has made you especially hungry, and you can ask for the last fish on the platter.

But remember: Save that bobber. You're going to be needing it again before the summer's over or I'll miss my bet!

T.S.

31

The Water-Drop Microscope

FROM THE vantage point of your tree house you might be able to see for miles. Peering into your catching jar, you can get nose to nose with a butterfly or moth or caterpillar. But how would you like to take a look at things too small to see with the naked eye?

You could buy a microscope like the ones in school. But let's make a microscope instead from a few simple materials, and use water for the lens. This project, like many others in this book, takes patience, experimentation, and is a great thing to do with your dad.

Here's the rudimentary scheme to make a water-drop microscope. Find the lid from a tin can and wash it off. With spray paint or a brush, paint one side of it black and let it dry. Then use a small nail (a brad) to poke a hole through the center

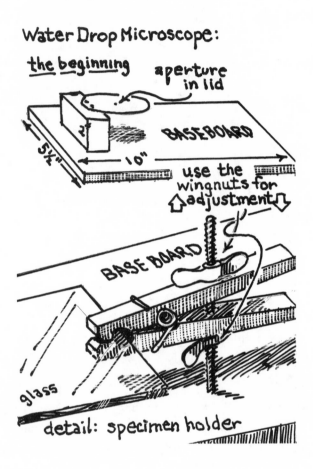

Water Drop Microscope:

the beginning   aperture in lid

BASEBOARD

5¼"   10"   2"

use the wingnuts for adjustment

BASE BOARD

glass

detail: specimen holder

of the unpainted side of the lid. Put a piece of scrap wood under the lid as you're doing this—don't use the tabletop. This hole is called an "aperture," and its size is critical for a successful microscope—so start with a very small hole, just penetrating the metal. You will notice that from the unpainted, shiny side of the lid, the hole sits in the middle of a small depression caused by the pressure that the hammer made on the nail before it penetrated the metal. That's the way it should be. That small depression is important.

Now use some wax, such as clear shoe polish, and wax the top (shiny) side of your can lid around the hole and down into the depression. By running a pin through the hole, make sure that the aperture is not plugged with wax.

Next, nail a two-inch-long block of wood to a piece of three-quarter-inch lumber that is about five and a half inches wide and ten inches long. Call this piece the "baseboard." Nail the block near one end of the baseboard using thin finishing nails so the block won't split. Then, using the fine nails (brads), nail the can lid, black-painted side down, by its edge to the block of wood. It will hang out away from the block. You will eventually be looking through the tiny aperture that you have made. The can lid is mounted so that you can do that.

At school the microscope has a mount for holding speci-mens. You must make something to place your specimens on so you can look at them. Take a spring-type clothespin and drill a hole with a three-sixteenth-inch drill through the ends of the clothespin as you press them together. Drill these holes about halfway to the position of the spring. This clothespin will hold your specimen glass, a rectangle of glass about one by two inches in size. You can get this glass, and many pieces like it, at the local glass store or at the hardware store. The "glass guy" will give them to you—scraps from replacing broken window panes that he will otherwise throw away. While he's cutting this glass, use your natural charm and ask him to cut the scrap of mirror you've brought with you into a square about one and a quarter inches. You can get a small piece of mirror almost anywhere—from an old makeup kit, a broken bathroom cabinet; or buy a little hand mirror at the dime store. Anyway, you need a square of one. Use a small piece of emery paper to smooth the edges of the glass and the mirror so you won't cut yourself.

And, while you're at the hardware store, pick up a stove bolt one-eighth by two and a half inches and three washers, one nut and two wing nuts to fit it. And buy a tube of silicone rubber cement as well.

Now, back to work. Assemble your specimen holder by inserting the narrow end of the piece of glass (the one-inch side) into the end of the clothespin. Lay this assembly down on the baseboard so that the glass is about centered under the aperture in the can lid. Make a mark on the baseboard with a finishing nail pushed through the holes you drilled in the clothespin. Set your specimen holder aside and drill a one-eighth-inch hole through the baseboard on the mark you just made.

Insert the stove bolt from the underside of the baseboard, place a washer on it, and then screw a nut down tight—tight enough to pull the head of the stove bolt into the baseboard. Now screw one wing nut, wings down, onto the installed stove bolt. Put on a washer. Place the specimen holder onto the stove bolt through the holes you drilled in it. Put on another washer and then screw on another wing nut, wings up.

A few words to explain this assembly: As with the microscope at school, you must be able to adjust the distance between the lens and the specimen to get a clear and precise view—this is called "focus." With the school microscope you change the distance between the lenses and the specimen, and between the lenses themselves. With the microscope that you are building, you can adjust the distance between the specimen and the lens. You do this by moving the wing nuts up or down the stove bolt. This will move your specimen holder up or down. The wing nuts don't have to be tight—just barely snug so you can swing your specimen holder out from under the aperture and then back under it, and it will be in the correct position.

One final part still must be made—the reflecting mirror that shines light up through the specimen-holder glass. That's why you had the glass guy at the hardware store trim your piece of mirror into a one-and-a-quarter-inch square. This mirror needs to be mounted diagonally under your aperture so it will reflect light upward. (You will shine the light in from the side.) You must mount the mirror under the aperture at a forty-five-degree angle above horizontal—that's halfway between being flat and being straight up. You can use a little block and some of the silicone cement to achieve this effect. Experiment with

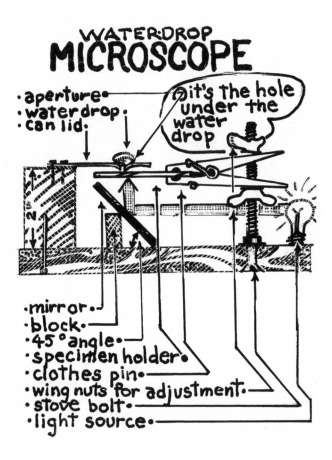

the placement; Make some marks so you can get back to the same place, remove the block and mirror, goop them up with the silicone and then put them back on the marks. Let the silicone dry.

The mounted mirror will be below your specimen holder,

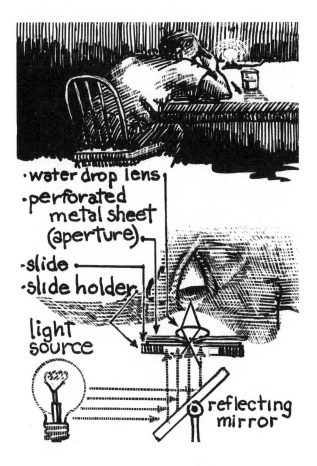

- water drop lens
- perforated metal sheet (aperture)
- slide
- slide holder

light source

reflecting mirror

which will swing in over the top of it. The whole microscope is now assembled!

The only thing that is missing is a lens. Getting one is this simple: Go to the sink and get a small glass of water. Using a medicine dropper, place one drop of water onto your aperture in the small depression created by punching the hole in the tin can lid. Remember you waxed it? That makes the water drop stand up, almost as a sphere. It flattens only slightly because of gravity, and will not fall through the aperture because the aperture is too small, and because of the surface tension of the water. (*Surface tension* is the attraction of the water molecules to one another; this is what causes the water to form into a drop to begin with.)

Why does the water make a lens? Because every transparent thing transmits light differently. As light passes from one transparent place to a different one—such as from clear air to clear water—the difference in the substance it is passing through causes the light to bend. The shape of the drop of water causes the light to bend all the way around the drop. The bending light intersects at a spot called its "focus."

When you're looking through the water drop at a very close distance from it, be careful that your eyelashes don't disturb it. You'll be looking through it at its focal distance. You'll know this is so, because what you'll see will become clear as you move your specimen holder up closer and closer to the bottom of the aperture. This part is trial and error. You will have positioned a light—a flashlight, for instance—to shine in from the side and reflect off of the mirror you mounted. That light will go through the clean glass of your specimen holder and through your specimen—the wing of a fly that you found dead on the windowsill, for instance. Then the light will be partly focused as it passes through the aperture—because that's what an aperture does. The light will be further focused by the water drop, and this will enlarge what you see. And there you have it! You are looking at tiny details that you could not otherwise see, not even with a magnifying glass.

One other thing: After the light goes through the water-drop lens it enters your eye through an aperture—the pupil in your eye—and then passes through another lens behind the pupil, and is focused again onto the retina of your eye so that you can see the image. It's all based on the same principle!

What other things can you look at? Pond water on your specimen-holder glass is a lot of fun to look at. It has tiny organisms living in it—mosquito larvae and such. Spiderwebs are fun to look at; feathers, caterpillar hairs, flower parts. So are crystals of salt and sugar.

When your lens starts to evaporate, dry off the aperture with a tissue and put another drop of water in place.

Sometimes you hear someone say: "Don't sweat the small stuff." True enough. Don't sweat it, but don't miss it either. It's a lot of what makes life interesting.

T.S.

32

Building a Tree House

TREES ARE very friendly beings. They house blackbirds and bees and chickadees. They welcome robins and crows and raccoons with bare toes. So why not us? We belong in trees. Some anthropologists* say our ancestors originated in trees. All I can remember about that is when I was a boy I thought trees had one purpose—to be climbed—and that God put them there for boys. What other legitimate purpose could you figure out for them, anyway?

So I climbed a lot of trees. Climbing up wasn't nearly as hard

*What do you think an anthropologist is? Is he someone who ap*ologizes* for having studied anthros? Some people think that man is a very sorry animal because he is greedy, wasteful and cruel. But I think that most people are good if they are given a chance to be good. Despite all of the foregoing, I think it would be a good idea to look up the word "anthropologist."

as getting down. You could climb until the limb up there started to sway, and your heart got to pounding, and you thought to yourself, "What kind of a dumb-bunny are you anyway to get yourself into this predicament?" Cats are like that too, you know. A dog can chase a cat up a tree and the cat can climb like crazy, and then the cat has a terrible time getting down again. But I do not think that our ancestors were cats—at least not mine.

Anyway, I always liked to climb trees better than I liked doing about anything else, unless it was fishing. That's where I learned tree hugging, because sometimes to climb a tree you have to hug it very hard and hold on with everything you've got in order to get up to the first branch where you can pull yourself up. This is called shinnying up a tree. You usually get your legs skinned a little on the rough bark, and sometimes your chest, but that's a small price to pay for the opportunity to get up into your pal, the tree.

After a while you get tired up there. Your feet get to hurting because they are stuck in a crotch and you get tired of holding on. Pretty soon you think, "Why don't I make a tree house here? A secret tree house." The reason that it will be a secret until you show it to somebody is because, if you notice, as people walk they usually do not look up. If I had a tree house here, I think, I could sleep in it overnight, or I could read a book up here, and no one could find me. I could make plans. I was always making plans— plans for going fishing, plans for going swimming. All kinds of plans. Or I could just lie back and enjoy being with the birds, and dream, which was what I liked to do best. I think birds dream a lot

because they hang out in the trees a lot, and trees are for dreaming.

I started looking around from up there where I was sitting in the crotch of the tree. The branches of that tree split so that they created three prongs, like the prongs that hold a gem in a ring. When you find a tree like that you have found a very special tree indeed, because although trees split as they go up, they usually do not split into three prongs—two, most often. So to build a tree house you have to find a tree that splits into at least three sturdy, alive prongs—alive, because if the prong is dead you can never tell how strong it is. It might be rotten at the core, and that is why it died, and you do not want to build a tree house or any house with a rotten foundation. Some time, when you least expect it, you might find yourself at the bottom of the tree before you intended to be there.

If you choose a three-pronged tree, your tree house is going to be in a triangle shape because you will secure boards, usually two-by-sixes, horizontally to the ground from prong to prong, and then over the two-by-sixes you will nail boards for the floor. If you can find a four-pronged tree, which is a real treasure, your floor will obviously be more square.

From what do you make this tree house? Finding the material is often as much fun as making the tree house. You can use old, solid fence rails, or you can find scrap lumber here and there. Maybe you will come on to a farm and see an old, dilapidated, falling-down shed behind the barn somewhere, and the farmer will let you take a few boards from it. It doesn't hurt to ask him. Tell him you want the lumber to build a tree house. As a boy he probably built a few himself. The worst he can say to you is no, which leaves you exactly where you were before you asked him, right? Tell him you will hoe his garden for the lumber. He'll never turn you down on that. Or you might have to go on a lumber search through the woods, and all of this could take some time. But who cares? You have all summer, and summers last approximately forever, don't they?

A person has to be very careful in building a tree house. You need a saw, a hammer and some nails. The nails have to be long enough to hold the two-by-sixes (or larger) that you use. A good test of adequate size is if it will hold Dad. Then it will obviously hold you. But Dad has to be careful as well. He can fall and break his head. Do you think you should bring a ladder into the woods to build it? Maybe you have to build the steps, like on Tom's drawing (see page 190), before you do anything else. But these steps can be dangerous, too. They can twist off, or give way. So the most important focus in building a tree house is how very careful you must be.

If you were native man building a tree house you wouldn't have any nails or any hammer. You would secure long tree limbs to the tree with vines. On this platform you would make a floor of other limbs and you wouldn't have any farmer around who you could talk out of some old lumber. But if you were native man you would be so very careful in climbing up the tree and making the house, because if you fell, you wouldn't have any hospital to go to to get a cast put on your leg or any doctor to set it. You would have to be what I would call super careful. And so must you and your dad be *super careful*, too. You will even want to build a rail around the platform so that you don't get careless and step off. If you can build a tree house without hurting yourself, you will have learned a lot about safety that will come in handy the rest of your life.

Tree houses are wonderful places to eat your lunch. Hardly anyone I know today eats his lunch in a tree. Lunches taste better up in trees for some reason that I have never been able to figure out. Maybe you can tell me. But it's so. And the air is a lot better up there than it is on the ground. When you get up there you will see that I am right. Besides that, you can see a lot farther from up in your tree house. You can see when the enemy is approaching so you can warn the other members of your tribe.

And up in a tree house you are safe from the marauding zoonots. They are called "zoonots" because they are not in the zoo. They are too horrible for people to look at in the zoo, and you can't catch them because they have five legs instead of four, and therefore they can run 20 percent faster than all other four-legged creatures. Zoonots do not have teeth, but they swallow you whole without chewing. So you do not want to get caught by a zoonot. That is one of the important reasons to build a tree house, because you are safe up there. Zoonots cannot climb trees. They cannot even see trees. They are what you call tree-blind. They go running through the forest bumping into tree after tree because they cannot see them. And that makes them

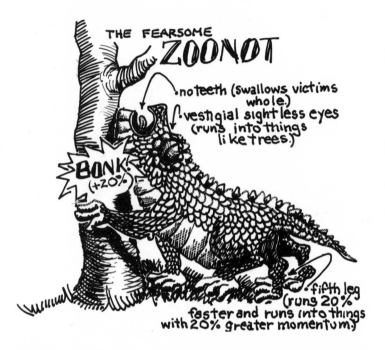

very mean. But the trees cannot see zoonots either. So that makes them even. In any event, you are always safe from zoonots in a tree house and that is something to know and remember.

And as you look out over the countryside from your high perch up in your tree house, you are the king—king of whatever and whomever you survey below. King of the ants, king of the gophers, king of the grasshoppers, king of almost everything. So the question is, will you be a good and kindly king, or a terrible tyrant? It is always up to you, O king up in the tree.

G.S.

33

Becoming a Poet

THE GREATEST of men have been poets. Shakespeare wrote poems. So did Jefferson. Lincoln wrote what I think was a very great poem—the Gettysburg Address. Christ told stories in poetic language, and the great speeches of Martin Luther King Jr. were really poems. If you are a poet you see things in a way that others do not see them. You feel things that others do not feel. And if you have this special sight, these magical feelings, your life will never become an empty bag.

Life is exploring who you are. Discovering who you are—that is, what lies hidden within you—is as exciting as exploring the woods at home and the jungles of foreign lands. Discovering who you are requires you to dig deeply for your feelings. Such is the way to true riches. The more feelings you discover and put in your bag, the richer you will become. I know many men who want to put only money in their bags. And although I think one needs money all right, the real riches of life are not money.

Becoming a poet is a way we learn about ourselves. A poem is merely the written words on a page that represent this discovery. To write a poem requires us to look inside ourselves and to record the feeling we have about the subject of our poem. A poem is not as much about thinking as about feeling. Let me give you an example.

Suppose it is springtime and we hear a bird singing. We could write, "I hear a bird singing. It sounds like a robin. Probably is because robins sing a lot in the springtime. I look out the window. I see the bird in the tree over there. It has a red breast, and a robin is the only bird I know that has a red breast in these parts of the woods." Now this is not a poem, or if it is, it is not a very good one because it contains only our thinking about what we have heard and seen.

But what if we use our head as a tool to call up the words that will express how we *feel*? To do this we must first focus into that part of us where we feel. We do not feel with our heads. We *think* with our heads and feel with our hearts. We feel our feelings somewhere in the body, in the chest, in the belly, in different places within the body depending upon the feeling we are having. If we are happy, the feeling may be higher in the chest than if we are afraid, which may be a feeling located lower in the chest. You might begin to notice exactly where in your body your feelings are located. Experiment. When you turn to something that makes you very joyous, where do you feel it? When you focus on something sad, where do you feel that? The next time you are angry, before you do or say anything, stop and ask yourself where in your body you are feeling the anger. To be aware of one's feelings is a precious gift. And when we become good at recognizing our feelings and know where they live in our bodies, we can also begin to write poetry.

Now, let us suppose that we hear this same bird singing. How does it make us feel? What does the feeling remind us of? Perhaps it reminds us of something as innocent and pure as a naked child. We could write, "A naked song exploded on my ears like children bursting from spring buds."

What does the song want us to do? What dreams does it call up? Listen to the feeling again. Can we locate the feeling in our bodies? The bird's song makes me want to fly with the music, but I am too old and stiff.

And what does the song say? Listen to the feeling again. Perhaps it says, "Be gay this one day, be light, and silly as bursting buds." (The song of the bird will likely say something quite different to you.) And then, thankful for the feeling, I might end the poem with my gratitude to the bird for its liberating song.

Now if we put it all together, I might have a poem:

SPRING SONG

A naked song
Exploded on my ears

Like children
Bursting from new buds.

And I
Too old
Too stiff to fly
On stony legs,
These featherless arms,
Can only wish
Can only cry.

Yet songs are victors in the end.
Songs capture age
And bend back
The heart.
Be free, they say,
Be gay,
Be light
And silly this one day
As thoughtless buds,

Thankful to this first spring bird,
Red breasted,
Ruby songed,
For one more featherless flight
Through wind and woods.

Poems are the music of words. They do not need to rhyme, although sometimes I use rhyming words if they come naturally, like: Be free they *say*. Be *gay* . . . this one *day*. Indeed, I think that looking for rhymes too often gets in the way of the feeling. But feelings are best expressed in the music and beat of the words, and the music needs to emerge in sounds and rhythm for the words to make a poem.

Do the sounds of the words you chose create the mood you want and reflect the feeling you had? Look for the sounds of what is called "alliteration," that is, words appearing close to each other that begin with the same letter—for example in my poem: *bursting . . . buds; featherless flight; wind and woods.*

Writing poetry is fun because it permits us to discover things about ourselves we did not know before. Before I wrote this poem I did not know it was stored away inside of me. And you do not know the poems that are waiting to be discovered by you. But I'll wager that you have many tucked away inside of you as well, all of which will come bursting forth (like new buds) whenever you're ready to feel them.

When you write a poem, others will begin to see you in a different light, because poets are usually seen as romantic, artistic, and as persons who have something interesting to say. Poets are people who offer something of themselves other than boring talk about the weather and the scores of the latest football games. Poets are valuable people.

I like to write poems out of doors, to sit down in the woods

and listen, to breath in the air and then write the feelings I have. You might observe an ant, and wonder how it is to be an ant. Are you also but an ant in this huge world? Some time you may wish to write about your feelings of love, or surprise, or delight, or sadness over the passing of a friendship. Writing poetry causes the person to grow within. It would be a tragedy, would it not, if we grew only on the outside?

When you and your dad are out together, bring along pencils and notebooks. Sit down on a rock or a log, and be silent. Silence lets you hear yourself. Listen. Listen carefully to the quiet sounds inside you and feel the feelings. Locate them in your body. Then begin to write, not what the head says, but what the feelings say. When you have finished your poem, read it to your father. And have him read his poem to you. You'll find something out about each other that you never knew before. It will be something beautiful. Something for each of you to put in your bags of life, something that is more valuable than all the money men can muster. Did you recognize the alliteration in the last sentence? Well, then, go write a poem of your own. And remember at last: your life is a poem, and you write it.

G.S.

About the Authors

Gerry Spence is a nationally renowned trial lawyer, author of many books, a television commentator on social issues, lecturer, teacher, photographer, father of six, and grandfather of ten. He lives with his wife, Imaging, in Jackson Hole, Wyoming.

Tom Spence—once a "serious artist" with fine arts degrees and a New York loft address to prove it—is now a dabbler. He is retired from a career underground working on the tracks in the New York City subways and serving as an officer in Local 100 of the Transport Workers Union. He is currently turning eggs at his diner on Main Street in Buffalo, Wyoming ... and fishing.

Get in touch with Gerry Spence at www.gerryspence.com.

Acknowledgments

Thank you to my brother, Gerry, for including me in this project that helped me remember being my father's son, and helped me be more my sons' father. And thanks to my sons—Taylor, who tied our own secret pattern of fly and helped cook the trout for the table, and Theo, who always reminds me it's never too early to get out the mitts and ball and begin spring practice. Thank you to my loving wife, Vikki, who has a larger heart than all the summers.

—Tom

Thank you to my brother, Tom. His drawings and inclusions, better than anything I could write alone, capture the magical spirit we both enjoyed in the cherished company of our father. Thank you to Bob Weil, my first editor at St. Martin's, who came up with the idea for this book as a result of his work with me in *The Making of a Country Lawyer,* and to Michael Denneny, my editor of late, who saw to this book's conclusion with the tenderness of an adopted parent. And thanks to John Sargent, the boss, who has been monstrously generous in permitting me to wander as I please, and to my agent, Peter Lampack, also my valued friend, who has always extended his hand when it has been most needed. Thanks to my sons, Kip, Kent, Brents, and Christopher, who have been patient and understanding as I have endeavored to learn the difficult skills of fatherhood. And, of course, thanks to my darling Imaging, who is at the nucleus of all that I ever do.   —Gerry